Undergraduate Education: Conflict and Change

Undergraduate Education: Conflict and Change

Arthur Sandeen
University of Florida

Lexington Books
D.C. Heath and Company
Lexington, Massachusetts
Toronto   London

Library of Congress Cataloging in Publication Data

Sandeen, Arthur.
    Undergraduate education.

    1. Education, Higher—United States. I. Title.
LA227.3.S26   378.73   75-41589
ISBN 0-669-00466-9

Published simultaneously in Canada.

Printed in the United States of America.

International Standard Book Number: 0-669-00466-9

Library of Congress Catalog Card Number: 75-41589

To My Parents

Contents

List of Figures

Preface

Debate over the form and content of undergraduate education in the United States dates back to 1636 and the founding of Harvard College. Should the emphasis in undergraduate academic programs reflect general education, vocational training, classical studies, personal and social values, religious enlightenment, or intellectual discipline? Vigorous proponents of each of these viewpoints continue the discussion about these issues, which have such an important influence upon higher education.

While this debate goes on, higher education in America has been confronted with an almost overwhelming array of pressures in recent years. Increased enrollments, emphasis upon research and publications, soaring costs, the drive for accountability, the competition for prestigious graduate programs, collective bargaining, statewide planning and budgeting—all these have combined to cause considerable confusion in academia. Undergraduate programs have often suffered as a result; they have become fragmented and do not reflect any well-understood educational philosophy. Undergraduate students on many campuses have not received adequate attention from senior faculty, and few institutions have consciously planned academic programs that had specific educational outcomes in mind.

The students themselves experience this confusion. While many of them have insisted upon practical courses that prepare them for jobs, this form of academic experience has left them feeling incomplete and frustrated.

Within this confusing scene, however, there is a positive climate for change. The mood for reform in undergraduate education is excellent. Out of the current atmosphere of conflict in undergraduate education, change is taking place. This book is intended to contribute to this process of change by suggesting positive actions that can be taken by institutions to develop undergraduate academic programs that can have an influence upon their students. The case description of the hypothetical "Segar University" in Chapter 5 is a specific illustration of how reforms can be incorporated into an institution. The chapters on undergraduate students and the impact of institutions are intended to demonstrate that there is a substantial amount of useful information available that institutions can use to strengthen their academic programs.

In writing a book of this nature, I have borrowed liberally from the ideas of many leaders in higher education. As a university administrator, professor, and an author, I am deeply indebted to Warren Bryan Martin, Kenneth Keniston, Harold Hodgkinson, Frederick Rudolph, Arthur

Chickering, Nevitt Sanford, and K. Patricia Cross for the many insights I have gained from their work over the years. Special gratitude is due to Stanley Lusby, Don James, and Robert Etheridge, who showed me how exciting undergraduate education can be.

Undergraduate Education:
Conflict and Change

1 The Current Status of Undergraduate Education

So long as instruction and life do not merge in our colleges, so long as what the undergraduates do and what they are taught occupy two separate airtight compartments in their consciousness, so long will the college be ineffectual (Wilson, 1925).

There has been a virtual explosion of growth in American higher education since 1960. The 8.5 million students enrolled in 1970 represented a 124 percent increase over the 1960 figure. The percentage of the population between the ages of 18 and 21 that was enrolled in degree credit programs in higher education increased from 23 percent in 1960 to 34 percent in 1970. In 1970 there were more than 2,800 institutions of higher education in the U.S., and three-quarters of the students attended public colleges and universities, as compared with only 60 percent in 1969. The most rapidly growing institutions in American higher education are the two-year colleges, whose enrollments increased by 71 percent between 1963 and 1970, to total 1,061. Their enrollment during this seven-year period tripled (Carnegie Commission, 1971). American higher education includes a wide diversity of types of institutions, such as community colleges, preparatory schools, liberal arts colleges, technical institutes, black colleges, land, sea, and urban grant universities, professional schools, research institutes, and doctoral-granting comprehensive "multiversities." Students in this vast system represent all economic levels of society, a wide range of academic ability and motivation, and a vast diversity of academic and professional goals. The United States has made the most dramatic commitment of any nation to the goal of providing equal access to higher education for its citizens. Eric Ashby, the noted British educator, has caught the spirit of American higher education quite accurately with the title of his excellent study for the Carnegie Commission, *Any Person, Any Study* (Ashby, 1971).

"Going to college" in American society became, during this period of time, an expected way of life, a required hurdle to clear for young people, and almost an unquestioned "article of faith" for a large portion of youth. Without question, one of the strongest motivating forces for young persons during this time has been the all-too-realistic notion that a college education was necessary both for economic survival and to get a decent job. The vocational nature of much of American higher education is well known, and the federal government itself has played a significant role in encouraging higher education for economic reasons by giving publicity to the higher

1

lifetime incomes of college graduates as compared with those of high school graduates. There does not seem to be as much perceived pressure on young persons to go immediately into a four-year college program, and there are more accessible and attractive job preparation opportunities through the vast community college system. "Career education" has now become a concept that is receiving a great deal of emphasis, especially from the federal government.

As is well known, higher education experienced tremendous difficulties as well as successes during this period. Indeed, it became the subject of national debate and filled front pages of news media and newscasts for a considerable period of time. Student unrest and dissatisfaction led, in many instances, to riots and take-overs; some campuses were viewed as "training grounds" for a new generation of activists who were antiwar, anticapitalistic, and anti-intellectual. The U.S. withdrawal from Vietnam, the ending of the draft, the state of the economy, and the disillusionment of many young persons following the 1972 election probably are major factors in the comparative calm that now exists on university campuses.

The tumultuous activities on American campuses during this period were perhaps more a reflection of the ravages in the larger U.S. and world society than they were unique events to higher education. Assassinations, riots in the cities, racial troubles, the Vietnam war, and political scandals made any attempt to establishing stability on the education scene impossible.

During this time, either consciously or unconsciously, many professors and administrators in higher education lost significant contact with their students. In having to concentrate on problems associated with huge enrollment increases, new building difficulties, the increasing explosion of knowledge, a dizzying pace of societal change, and faculty and student unrest, the fundamental nature of the undergraduate educational experience changed significantly. Although there is no misconception in this book that undergraduate education was "correct" or ideal in the past, much of it during this period became impersonal, fragmented, vocational, unreflective of any integrated philosophy or purpose, and perhaps most striking of all, unrelated to the personal lives of students. The current emphasis on "career education" may satisfy the nervous anxieties of many parents, legislators, and administrators about the job market and enrollment problems, but it is, in the words of Earl McGrath (1974), a "time-bomb" for society. He argues that the survival of our culture is at stake, and to pursue professional competence and technocratic efficiency without maintaining an active concern for values would be disastrous.

The purposes of this book are: to assess the current crisis in undergraduate education, to outline some of the factors that had led to this situation, to describe in part the impact of colleges upon student lives, and to suggest some new directions for undergraduate education that may help relate more effectively the academic content of higher education to the lives of students.

Undergraduate education in the United States today is badly fragmented; it lacks a coherent overall philosophy, it needs a strong and enlightened leadership, and it affects too little the very people it is meant for—the students. The agendum for many colleges and universities has been so sidetracked by problems and crises during the past fifteen years that too often the undergraduate curriculum and the students themselves have been ignored, or "put off until later." Although there were notable exceptions, too often the experience of this undergraduate at a large public urban university was not uncommon:

When I arrived at the university as a freshman, I suspect I was very typical—I was scared, but eager. I immediately became involved in a seemingly endless hassle of mechanical and administrative hurdles—from admissions itself to the registration process, financial aid, housing—even payment of the dorm fees. Although I was completely undecided about what I wanted to major in, there was no one around except a few guys in the dorm who I could talk to about it. I found myself in a bunch of courses my first year that I selected without knowing anything except what I read on an instruction sheet and asked a secretary about. Some of the courses turned out okay, but I had two taught by TAs who really were bad news. The second semester was almost as bad, but at least by then, I had figured out pretty well what the system was—take whatever you want, as long as you get the requirements, and they won't hassle you. I've done this for over three years now, just like most students, but now I realize, I guess too late, that I've really missed a lot. I don't even know any professors well, and they sure as hell don't know me. I changed my major three times, so now I'm looking for a teaching job. There never seemed to be any rhyme or reason to what I was doing here—it was just a bunch of courses that satisfied the requirements, and added up to the right total. I took a lot of exams, and passed the courses, but what the hell difference did it make? Maybe it will all make some sense to me a couple of years from now.

Factors Affecting Undergraduate Education

There are many institutional factors that have operated at cross purposes with a coherent program in undergraduate education. One of the most critical—and least examined—is size. Little evidence exists that indicates that there is any ideal size for an institution, whatever its purposes; and the current "caps" on total enrollment at various state institutions in California, Illinois, and Florida reflect more biases of state planners and legislators than any educational evidence on the matter. However, institutions that have experienced drastic enrollment increases in the past fifteen years too often have not made corresponding adjustments in their academic programs for students. Too many institutions have continued to expand existing programs and procedures that serve the needs of 3,500 students, but not 16,000 students. Many professors simply have not had the time, or the inclination, to visit personally with 65 to 100 students each semester during the registration process; and many undergraduates have found it more critical to "get through the maze" than to visit with a professor about their plans and problems. Size has contributed to the feeling of impersonality experienced by many students. As a student personnel administrator for over fifteen years, I have been asked many times to write letters of recommendation for graduating seniors who reported that there were no faculty whom they could ask, because no faculty knew them or anything about them. When this happened the first time, my reaction was one of disbelief, but it has been repeated often enough that I know the situation is real.

In the 1960s, some students began to react against this impersonality, as the strong words of Jeffrey Elman (1967) illustrate:

Students today . . . want a university which is personally and socially committed. Instead of this commitment, students find the university clinging to the vocationalism and specialization of the Morrill Act. . . . They find that they have become receptacles, expected to sit in the lecture hall and receive what their professors exude.

These reactions to the impersonality of institutions went far beyond mere procedures. In many ways, the reactions were against the educational program itself, the content of which was often termed irrelevant by the students or was seen as something apart from their everyday lives. Large, lecture-type classes, taught by a professor who could not possibly know the names of the 250 students in the auditorium, much less anything about them, are not a stimulating and integrating learning model for most students. Objective, machine-scored examinations that give no opportunity for personal criticism or student-faculty dialogue can further depersonalize the undergraduate experience. Although many faculty have been willing to spend long hours with students in academic advising, too often even these contacts are largely concerned with the mechanics of course requirements.

Increasingly students were viewed as consumers of a product that was marketed, Madison Avenue style, rather than as active participants in their own education or in the governance process itself. Due to the emotion-charged nature of student demands during this period, many institutions included students on policy-recommending boards, curriculum committees, and search and screen committees. However, at large institutions this "student involvement" was little more than token participation for a few activists or student government aspirants, and it had little effect on the daily educational lives of the great majority of students. Clark Kerr's "Multiversity" became synonymous with impersonality, a symbol against which students could rally. At some of these very large universities, the size and impersonality of the institution made "The Lonely Crowd" a reality. Kerr (1963) wrote about what a confusing place the university can be with its vast range of choices, and he referred to its high "casualty rate" and its many "walking wounded."

One notable example of combatting the overwhelming size problem was Michigan State University's effort to "grow large while remaining small," in John Hannah's words (1967), through the creation of smaller, decentralized academic units on the campus. Each of these "cluster colleges" (also tried elsewhere) developed a distinctive academic mission, and they selected faculty and students in accordance with a well-documented purpose. Facilities and administrative arrangements were made sufficiently attractive to accommodate the academic purposes of the colleges effectively. Each college was to remain small (750 to 1,000 students) so that a close student-faculty identity could be established, while both students and faculty could, at the same time, benefit from the substantial academic and extracurricular offerings at the larger, "parent" university. While these cluster colleges have not drastically affected the structure of undergraduate education for all students at Michigan State, they have offered a stimulating and coherent alternative for students who elect to participate.

Size in itself does not have to be debilitating to students or destructive of a well-defined and clearly understood educational program. But unless the institution takes aggressive and creative steps to personalize the university to its students, and unless it continuously presents evidence of its goals and educational objectives, students will probably not perceive much purpose or meaning in their undergraduate progress.

Decline of General Education

The growing absence of general education programs in four-year institutions has contributed significantly to the lack of coherence in undergraduate education. Daniel Bell (1966) uses strong words to describe the trend:

What one sees today is the falling apart of general education and its replacement by a cafeteria system whereby any and every kind of course is admitted within the corpus, so long as a student takes some—or any—courses outside his specialization. . . . The hopes of interdisciplinary integration, so high 20 years ago, have not materialized, at least on the general education level.

Sir Eric Ashby, the perceptive and respected British educator, as a member of the Carnegie Commission, observed in his study, *Any Person, Any Study* (1971) that

General education . . . was a courageous concept: to introduce the undergraduate to the rudiments of the whole of man's intellectual heritage through surveys or selected episodes of thought. But it does not appear to have succeeded. The view that it succeeded but is now no longer necessary owing to improvements in secondary school curricula is not convincing. Even at its best (as at Harvard) general education has disappointed its creators; and at its less than best (e.g., the Plato-to-Sartre in twenty hours sort of course held in some large state universities and taught by televised lectures and teams of graduate instructors) it may be counter productive, for it provides information without understanding, and this is liable to destroy a student's intellectual self-confidence. It is better to be ignorant than to have undigested knowledge lumbering one's mind.

If general education programs have not succeeded, and if the "undergraduate curriculum" is little more than a cafeteria, then institutions have not really considered these issues as high priorities, but have succumbed to the process of specialization and departmentalism. By allowing students to select virtually any courses as long as they meet the narrow and specialized requirements for a specific major indicates to students that the institution doesn't have any real, overall educational mission except to train students for a narrow profession. Moreover, it speaks most loudly to undergraduates as it virtually ignores them as persons—students know they don't matter as much as the mechanical and content-related nature of the course requirements.

There are indications (e.g., Feldman and Newcomb, 1969) that much of the change that takes place in a student's attitudes, values, and learning styles occurs in the first two years of college. Yet it is precisely here that too many universities spend the least amount of time with and have the least commitment to students. Harold Hodgkinson (1971) indicates that the curriculum of the first two years of college is very weak, and that the high attrition rate is the result, at least partially, of ineffective programs during the first year. The programs, he argues, are difficult to change because most of the faculty are not interested in them.

Students of any age are not easily fooled, and most undergraduates learn all too quickly that the "real action" at the university is not in the first- and second-year classrooms. Frequently, those who arrive at universities as enthusiastic and eager first-year students are "turned off" to the learning process and to the institution by the absence of a thoughtful, stimulating curriculum, and by faculty whose priorities are elsewhere.

Emphasis upon Graduate Programs

The temptation to create graduate programs almost overnight has been too great for many institutions of higher education to resist in the past fifteen years. Many colleges, public and private, primarily for reasons of prestige and to attract and retain outstanding faculty, developed master's and doctoral programs in a wide variety of disciplines, sometimes despite inadequate facilities, personnel, and financial resources. Too often, this resulted in lower priority being given to undergraduate programs.

Ashby (1971) argues that while the graduate school has many outstanding accomplishments, it is costly and is likely to impoverish the undergraduate program. Its success may have some negative effects upon other segments of the institution.

Moreover, on many campuses that developed large and diverse graduate programs, there existed a well-known and cynically referred to "pecking order" among the students themselves. Undergraduates too often viewed themselves, especially as first- or second-year students, as almost "unworthy" of the time or concern of professors. It was clearly implied on the campus that graduate students (especially those on the Ph.D. level) were the "preferred clientele" since they alone, of course, were capable of doing research, dealing with the really weighty issues, or attending faculty meetings. Indeed, this writer has observed many undergraduates who sincerely apologize to faculty for "taking their time" and others who have felt genuine guilt over having "interrupted faculty's work."

There is no attempt here to make a case for a deemphasis upon graduate education, nor is any implication intended that graduate programs are not critical to higher education and society in general. Indeed, the quality of an undergraduate program can be enormously enhanced and enriched by the presence of strong graduate programs. On campuses where there are outstanding graduate departments, undergraduate students should be able to benefit significantly from the more sophisticated facilities, equipment, research, library, faculty, and graduate students themselves. The undergraduate program, however, needs to reflect a clear-cut mission of its own, so that students and faculty understand its goals and educational purpose.

Emphasis upon Research and Publications

In his important study for the Carnegie Commission, *Institutions in Transition* (1971), Harold Hodgkinson noted that as the comprehensiveness of a school increases, the commitment toward teaching decreases. With the striking growth and expansion of institutions in the past fifteen years, it is not surprising that undergraduate teaching programs have suffered from lack of attention. Although there is evidence that larger percentages of faculty are now being granted tenure than before, and that it is being granted earlier in one's academic career (Hodgkinson, 1971), there is still a very strong emphasis upon research and publications in the faculty scramble for promotion. The cliché "publish or perish" is still quite valid, especially in the perceptions of many undergraduate students at large, research-based universities. There is more prestige involved for faculty to be concerned with research projects and "their own work" than with the educational and personal lives of undergraduates. Moreover, the rewards to faculty in terms of promotion, salary increases, a professional reputation are clearly based on the research, publications, and national exposure they can produce, not on undergraduate teaching. Clearly, some professors are openly bored with the "low-level content" of undergraduate courses, and they are tired of having to listen to the "sophomoric concerns and identity crises of these students." There are many other faculty, however, who are genuinely interested in undergraduate students and are inspiring teachers as well, but who are torn between their dedication to the needs of these students and the administration's demands to produce research and publications in professional journals. This emphasis upon reputation, rewards, and money has taken many professors further away from undergraduates in their consulting roles. Faculty represent expertise in a great variety of activities, of course, and many are frequently called to other campuses, corporations, the state and federal governments, school systems, and other countries. This consulting activity has been actively sought out by faculty, as it can enhance their professional advancement, prestige, and pocketbooks. Too often, however, it means yet another reason why undergraduates may not get much attention from outstanding faculty. As Clark Kerr (1963) has argued, many of the changes that have taken place in universities have separated faculty members from students, and the revolt that used to be against the faculty *in loco parentis* is now against the faculty *in absentia*.

Research, writing, and professional consultation are not at all incompatible with undergraduate teaching. Moreover, a faculty member at a modern university most likely is not growing and learning in his/her field if he or she is not actively engaged in at least one of these activities. There are many nationally prominent full professors who, while being involved in significant research activity, also interact frequently with undergraduate students, in and out of the classroom. Indeed, they make better and more concerned teachers because they bring to undergraduates their own sense of excitement with their research and they find ways to involve these students in the problems and issues raised by their ongoing projects. Research activity has tended too often to separate faculty from undergraduate teaching and advising, and it has isolated some faculty from ongoing contacts with the concerns and needs of these students. Although the reward systems in higher education have encouraged faculty to work in those directions, undergraduate teaching can be revitalized and integrated with these professional concerns of the faculty. At the present time, in many institutions students are "left to their own devices" in their academic programs, and the only persons with whom they ever spend much time in a serious consideration of the content of their work are other students.

Although there are obvious benefits to this, the process of higher education must be more meaningful and involved with faculty. For many students, due to this isolation from faculty, Stanley Heywood's (1971) observation that higher education can "indeed be a very dull experience" is too often a reality.

Growing Departmentalization

The only link that the separate schools and departments at a university have, it has been said, is that they share a central heating system! Kerr (1963) has revised this slightly; he views the university as a series of individual faculty entrepreneurs held together by a common grievance over parking!

Warren Bryan Martin (1968) argues that our interest in educating the whole person is inconsistent with our academic specialization. He claims that universities

cut off the student's head from his body and have it dissected according to the specialties of various departments, while the victim's body is allotted to student personnel services.

Although well over one-half of all students on many campuses change their academic major at least once, and many more than once, there is a growing tendency among institutions to assume that students, even in their first year, are (or ought to be) firmly committed to a professional field, and should begin a structured, predetermined, and unswerving program to that end. Much of the structure of undergraduate programs today reflects more of the specialized approach of a graduate curriculum than the broad-based one of the undergraduate program. Students are painfully aware of the penalties involved if they deviate too far from the prescribed departmental requirements. If they "get out of sequence" (one of the major sins that can be committed), they may graduate a semester late, miss good job opportunities, increase their own costs, or incur the disapproval of faculty and parents. To many students today, the term "elective" is a standing, cynical joke. Their curriculum may be so proscribed that their only "electives" are available in their last two years, and then these must comprise "no more than 5 percent of the total program." One college catalog indicates that students must enroll for at least 9 credits of "sociohumanistic studies," as part of their overall program of 192 credits. Whatever "sociohumanistic studies" are is anyone's guess, but the implication that taking 9 credits in such academic activity constitutes a "broadening of the educational experience" is both an insult to the academic integrity of the faculty and an illustration of the lack of coherence in undergraduate education. The department reigns supreme. The power and autonomy of academic departments in higher education are a reason both for the academic achievements of institutions and for their shortcomings. It is only a very courageous and innovative dean who can make many inroads into the departments and alter or broaden the scope of their concerns. Students enrolled in "their department" become "their students," and in recent years departments have protected and clung to their students for more than academic reasons—the number of students enrolled in the discipline may have a direct impact upon the funding of its programs and the support for its faculty. Students unknowingly become pawns in interdepartmental power and money struggles; and, of course, the lack of any comprehensive and sensible approach to undergraduate education is clearly reflected.

This writer recently attended a meeting for retired professors on a large university campus and heard a professor of English comment, "You know, there are buildings on this campus that I've never been in. I've never been in mechanical engineering, chemistry, or physics." The professor then pointed out that he had taught on that campus for thirty-five years. Others then joined the discussion, which became quite lively and humorous. Several other retired faculty indicated that they, too, had never even stepped inside various campus buildings "not associated" with their discipline. In a serious and provocative discussion that followed about the educational program, there was a general consensus that "something had been lost" in this rather isolated arrangement, and that the quality of the undergraduate program had undoubtedly suffered because they really had never pushed themselves to develop interdisciplinary and cross-departmental programs. The group was also disappointed to discover that several among them had not been in a student residence hall or fraternity or sorority house to visit with students in almost twenty years.

It is too often assumed that once a student enrolls in a particular department, she or he is not only going to graduate in that discipline, but will also either pursue graduate studies in that area or obtain a job in that field and stay in it for a long time. The actual behavior of students and graduates, of course, does not follow this pattern. Large numbers of students take jobs immediately after college that are not directly related to their undergraduate majors—and more striking, the mobility in the work force now is such that most persons change jobs several times, so that five years after graduation, many are in positions essentially unrelated to their undergraduate concentration. Yet too many institutions continue to increase the narrow and preprofessional nature of their academic programs. Aside from the fact that these approaches do not represent any logical, broad-based educational philosophy, the ironic result is that students are not well served even for their narrow professional purposes, due to their own shifts in academic and professional preferences.

Students, of course, have contributed to this emphasis upon departmentalism by their own insistence on 'relevance" and their own academic myopia. All professors have heard students complain about, "why do I have to learn this?—It's not related to what I'm going to do." Too often, faculty departments and institutions have reinforced such attitudes with the overemphasis upon course work as preparation for a job. The current fad for "career education" being pushed by the federal and state governments can only enhance this trend and further the fragmentation of undergraduate programs.

The academic department is a great strength in American higher education. It has become too autonomous and isolated, however, and too free to control a large part of the curriculum for undergraduate students. Strong leadership is needed to develop programs in undergraduate education that take advantage of the strengths of departments with imaginative new arrangements of curricula, facilities, and faculty.

Institutional Governance

In recent years, due largely of course to the student protests, institutions have made adjustments in their committee structures, admitting some (usually small numbers) students to the consideration of issues as diverse as parking and residence hall rules to curriculum requirements and the selection of faculty. Even though this "participation" by students in institutional governance has been largely token in nature, and most undergraduates do not seem overly concerned with such matters, the overall results of this student participation have been more positive then negative. Many students, by such participation, have learned a great deal about their university, its goals, and its problems; and they have benefited most of all, perhaps, from their interaction with faculty members in new settings. In some cases, students have made substantial contributions to the process. They have also learned that not all university business is as exciting and romantic as they perhaps initially thought, and too often, as a result, students have withdrawn in boredom or frustration. They have learned about the difficulty of making significant changes in social institutions, and perhaps something about their own abilities and ideas as they are scrutinized by others in open discussions.

When students and faculty have been able to work together in real tasks that have some chance of actual implementation, a greater sense of community has been created, and the quality of academic life for both has been enhanced. When students feel that they can make a difference, that their ideas may have some merit, or that they are considered contributing members of the organization, their commitment to and identity with the institution will most likely be enhanced (Berelson and Steiner, 1964). Too few students have such opportunities, however, even at institutions that make substantial and sincere efforts in these directions. Moreover, the attitude that the faculty and the administration project toward students is perhaps more important than the actual administrative arrangements or committee structure. James Kunen (1968) expressed the sentiments of many undergraduates on this issue in his book, *The Strawberry Statement*:

"A university is definitely not a democratic institution," Professor Deane began, "When decisions begin to be made democratically around here, I will not be here any longer. Whether students vote 'yes' or 'no' on an issue is like telling me they like strawberries."

Even though a student's opinion on a particular issue may not be the most sophisticated or defensible one, the institutional "climate" has a good deal to do with how likely it is that a student will express it and have it listened to. If the institution views its students as merely passive "consumers," then their participation in the governance process and their own thoughts and feelings about their experiences will probably not be viewed as very important. Most importantly, the students themselves will not feel a part of the educational community, as they perceive that their own ideas and contributions are viewed officially as having little value.

Some substantial efforts have been made in recent years to change and improve governance structures, to achieve a greater sense of participation and sense of community on the campus, and to improve the overall educational program. The development of broad-based university senates, tripartite commissions, and ad hoc task forces has been quite extensive, although the results of such arrangements are mixed at this time. Various research instruments now exist (e.g., Educational Testing Service, 1972) that enable a campus to measure its own sense of community, its "openness," as perceived by students and faculty. Predictably, there are wide institutional differences in this regard, and campuses would be wise to assess their current "environment" and to make efforts to affect it in ways consistent with their educational objectives.

Perhaps the most significant factor involving institutional governance within the past fifteen years has been the development of new state "coordinating" boards of higher education. As Hodgkinson (1971) points out in his study of institutions, external authorities are wielding more and more power over campus affairs, and the autonomy that used to be taken for granted is declining. Instead of being able to consider their own problems and priorities as independent institutions, now many state universities are parts of "state systems," with their roles defined either by the legislature or by a "superboard." Increasingly, this has meant a loss of autonomy and a lessening of institutional distinctiveness. Too often it has also meant that the crucial decisionmakers are no longer the faculty, students, and administration on the campus itself, but are board members, legislators, and distant educational bureaucrats in a state office. In some states, there seems to be an obsession with uniformity of procedures and rules for all the state campuses, and there are indications that this may soon include academic matters as well, such as the proposed ''common-course-numbering system'' for the state institutions in Florida. Changes in curriculum, institutional mission, and even academic procedures are very difficult to achieve in these new bureaucratic systems. Faculty, students, and even top administrators may conclude, with some correctness, that their roles in governance are primarily custodial in nature, and that they are simply to execute policy and academic programs as directed by outside agencies. The academic consequences of this situation are disastrous for the individual campuses, their sense of vitality, and their own freedom to create and experiment with new programs. These academic straitjackets placed on the campuses may result in constrictions on the initiative of institutions to develop integrated, broad-based undergraduate programs, and may drive faculty further into their departments out of frustration and a need for security.

There are very justifiable financial and educational reasons, of course, for sensible and enlightened statewide planning and coordination of public higher education. There has been unwise and uneconomical duplication of academic programs at several levels within states, and there are increasingly limited resources available for higher education. Taxpayers have every right to have their educational dollars distributed in an efficient manner that best serves the interests of all persons in the state. State coordinating boards and legislatures do not have to put harnesses upon institutions, however, or muzzle their voices. Instead of being a barrier and a hindrance to the development of distinctive and lively undergraduate programs, they can be helpful stimulants to these processes and programs. They need to recognize the nature of a university and the very real needs of each institution to feel that it is doing something unique and important, and that it has, in fact, created this itself. Education, in its most effective and vital form, is not some neutral, inert, body of information that is stoically passed on by faculty to the students. It is a constantly growing, dynamic set of interactions and daily discoveries that are created by faculty and students together. Unless the campus itself perceives that it has these opportunities as an independent, self-sustaining, and internally responsible enterprise, it is not at all likely that much is going to happen to develop a coherent educational program. Students and faculty should be accountable to each other because they have created together the objectives, form, and content of their educational programs. Their own sense of investment in and concern for the outcomes is enhanced in this manner. However, if both are simply "fulfilling someone else's requirements," then the sense of institutional mission is gone and the vitality of the educational experience is greatly diminished.

The Emergence of Collective Bargaining

As noted in the final report of the Carnegie Commission (1973a),

Collective bargaining is now spreading rapidly, although its future course is quite unclear. It now covers about 15 percent of the professoriate, mostly in community colleges and in comprehensive colleges and universities; it has penetrated little as yet into liberal arts colleges and research universities. It can come, when it does, as a supplement to current forms of governance, if it is confined to bargaining over matters of compensation; or it can be a totally new form of governance, as in the Boston State contract, covering all decision-making processes. Half or more of faculty members, according to our studies, now favor collective bargaining, and also favor greater militancy in asserting faculty interests.

"Asserting faculty interests" is perhaps the key phrase in this paragraph that can work at cross purposes to efforts to develop a broad-based, revitalized undergraduate curriculum. Faculty interests can include teaching and advising loads, class size, research opportunities, involvement in policy decisions, tenure regulations, and salaries, among others. Each of these is very important; but if faculty members become so preoccupied with their own security and working conditions, they may tend to become separated from issues central to the campus's educational program, and the sense of community that exists may be eroded. Collective bargaining places professional members of the academic community into a labor-management relationship and emphasizes a "we-they" conflict between faculty and administration, or, increasingly, between the institution and the governing board. Dialogue among colleagues can be replaced by negotiation, and the emphasis upon various campus "power groups" may become enhanced. The arbitration process may polarize campus groups on various issues, while distant "representatives" argue in formal, legalistic terms one "side's" case against the other.

In the Carnegie Commission report on *Governance in Higher Education* (1973a), it is argued that collective bargaining will result in a reduction of campus autonomy, because the people with the money (in state institutions) are the legislators and governors. Negotiations will most likely be with these groups, and federal and state employee relations boards will decide such issues as the composition of the bargaining unit and the various matters subject to bargaining. Professional arbitrators may rule on various disputes and grievances. There also may be impacts upon interdepartmental uniformity, on flexibility of treatment of individual faculty cases, and on the tone of the relationships with administrators and trustees.

The governance process itself may be changed significantly depending on the nature of the contract. Faculty and administrative roles may become carefully proscribed, and informal and spontaneous relationships may decrease. Perhaps of greatest concern, collective bargaining raises several bothersome issues regarding undergraduate students and the educational program. If faculty interests "are paramount in a particular contract, most likely students do not have any significant role in the governance process." In effect, some collective bargaining agreements "write out" students from the governance process altogether, or "allow them" only a token "observer" role. Previous gains that students had made regarding involvement in campus issues can be eliminated. More importantly, the perceptions students have of their acceptance as participating members of the academic community can be greatly diminished. If faculty members and others on the campus have been stating their "commitments to undergraduates and their fine contribution to the governance process," then these statements quickly become hollow rhetoric to the students. A sense of community can quickly become a sense of cynicism. In extreme situations, where faculty may actually go on strike, students may become embittered toward their professors, now convinced that "when the chips are down, the faculty take care of themselves first, and the hell with the students." The need for broad-based reform in undergraduate education may not be enhanced by the presence of collective bargaining. Instead of being concerned with campuswide educational programs for students that may involve the "breaking down" of departmental barriers, faculty may further isolate themselves into their own departments, secure with the contents of their contract.

Collective bargaining can be viewed, however, as a positive force within the educational community if it serves to ensure appropriate professional roles for faculty, and if it does not remove campus groups from playing a meaningful role in governance. It can function to maintain effective class sizes, teaching and advising loads, fair and equitable procedures for faculty evaluation, and adequate financial compensation for faculty, all of ,which may serve the cause of effective educational programs and campus morale very well. By giving a clearer definition of faculty responsibilities, professors may eventually be more free to participate in efforts to create more vital educational options for students. In some cases, of course, the rights of faculty, their prerogatives to determine the curriculum, and the work loads they actually undertake have been abridged or arbitrarily determined. Collective bargaining has the potential in some situations to ensure fairness, and perhaps to protect vital educational principles. There probably has not yet been enough experience in American higher education with collective bargaining to evaluate fairly its impact upon students, the governance process, the institutional climate for experimentation, or the development of new and clearly articulated educational options for undergraduates.

Collective bargaining is now a major issue on many campuses, and faculty, students, administrators, board members, and legislators would do well to consider together its probable impact upon their institution. Ladd and Lipset (1973) have speculated that faculty unionism will be a storm center in the future, and although it has been viewed with disdain by many professors over the years, it will become a major issue for institutions. The consequences for the future of higher education in this country may be very serious.

Soaring Costs of Education

While total enrollments and total revenues from states and the federal government have increased dramatically during the past fifteen years, the soaring increases in the costs of higher education have placed severe burdens on many institutions. Especially for some private institutions, but also for growing numbers of public colleges and universities as well, financial cutbacks and decreasing numbers of students have meant difficult retrenchment. A few institutions have closed, others have merged, and some have significantly limited the scope of their programs in order to balance their books. The skyrocketing cost of living, rampant inflation, the almost prohibitive cost of new construction, faculty's increasing salaries, costs of other labor essential to the operation of the institution, and a depressed economy have combined to make institutions' efforts to stay out of the red a highly critical matter. Tuition charges have been increased dramatically during the last fifteen years, and the gap between tuition at most private universities and public institutions has increased significantly. The financial burden placed upon a student and his/her family now for a four-year college education can easily reach $20,000 and more. Clearly, many families cannot afford these costs, and increasingly they are questioning the value of the investment. The costs of higher education have become part of a national debate and the subject of present items on prime-time national television such as the CBS News documentary, "Higher Education: Who Needs It?" In this program, students, parents, faculty, and legislators are interviewed, and the message comes through clearly in the form of a question: "Why are so many students and their families investing so much money to get a college education when it may not get them a job anyway?" This plain talk to the public about the function of higher education as job preparation, especially when emphasizing the enormous financial sacrifices involved, can be very persuasive.

Many private institutions that are in financial difficulty face a seemingly unrelenting dilemma. In order to compete with public institutions, they need to keep their tuition as low as possible and offer a wide range of educational programs. Yet, as their student enrollment declines (upon which they depend so heavily for income), they are forced to raise tuition, lower their educational standards, or cut back their educational offerings, all of which may work at cross purposes to their efforts to survive. This "vicious cycle" can virtually destroy an institution, as it struggles to define its priorities and options.

There appears to be some erosion in the long-standing assumption in this country that society is the great benefactor of a well-educated public, and thus should make efforts to place as few barriers as it can in the way of its young people seeking an education. Although the total dollars invested in higher education by the public are very great, students themselves are now having to assume a greater responsibility for the actual costs of education, and thus are increasingly viewed as the primary benefactors of it. This highly disturbing trend may work at cross purposes with national efforts to achieve equal access to higher education, and may discourage many young persons from pursuing a higher education. The Carnegie Commission (1973a) has itself suggested that students should assume a greater proportion of the costs of higher education, and this kind of recommendation undoubtedly will influence state planners and legislators concerned with financing higher education.

There has been significant growth, of course, in the development of federal and state programs in financial aid to students, and generally these programs have assisted the country in its efforts to provide more equal educational opportunity. However, the administration of these programs has been uneven, and some institutions have been able to benefit more than others. With the costs of higher education soaring, there is an increasing level of frustration among middle-class Americans, who may perceive themselves as not having sufficient access to federal and state financial aid programs, and having to borrow heavily to send their children to college. The ambitious goals of the Basic Grants Program have not been more than partially realized to date, and a growing number of educators are looking to the federal government to expand its role in funding institutions.

In some instances, colleges that have faced difficult financial problems and declines in their enrollment have resorted to "hard-sell" admissions practices, and they have compromised the integrity of their academic programs and standards in efforts to survive. But education cannot be packaged and marketed, Madison Avenue style, without large numbers of students and parents becoming very distrustful. Students and others quickly learn the gap between promise and delivery, and such practices, besides being unethical, are counterproductive to the institution.

The Carnegie Commission's report on *The More Effective Use of Resources* (1972) deals with the difficulties many institutions face in their fiscal operations. In the report, it is argued that the current financial crisis is the most serious one faced by American higher education. This difficult situation must be accepted, and real adjustments must be made. Despite the financial pressure, however, the report urges institutions to target from 1 to 3 percent of their budgets for reforms and new programs.

The cost squeeze may cause some institutions to be overly cautious in their educational planning and experimentation, convincing them that the most secure course is to avoid making major reforms as long as the "ship is not sinking." New curricular arrangements, new facilities, and new programs can be expensive; and a discouraging outcome of financial retrenchment can be a severe cutback on innovation at a time when it is perhaps needed the most.

On the other hand, financial exigencies may actually force institutions to evaluate their programs, priorities, and use of resources in ways not done before, perhaps resulting in a more clearly stated institutional mission, a more understandable and sensible set of curricular offerings, and a new sense of community among faculty, students, and staff. Too many institutions, in an effort to be "all things to all people," have found that this is not possible or even desirable. Some now have instead decided to emphasize their own distinctiveness in style, program emphasis, and tradition; and they have sought to attract students and faculty who are compatible with these more limited, and possible, goals. American higher education has long prided itself on institutional diversity; yet in the past fifteen years there has been a tendency for institutions to become more alike. The current difficult financial situation may serve as an uncomfortable stimulus for institutions to develop new and creative programs, thus increasing the diversity of educational programs available for students, and contributing to the distinctiveness of the total system.

Program Budgeting

As states have allocated more and more dollars for higher education, and as legislators, state planners, and others increasingly have emphasized financial efficiency and "cost effectiveness" in universities, new methods of determining the needs of campuses have been developed and used. Program Planning Budgeting Systems, or "PPBS," has become a reality at many universities, and various management techniques from business and the federal government have increasingly been applied to higher education.

Funds have been allocated to universities by counting the number of "student credit hours" produced by enrollments at various academic levels and applying this information to a formula. Faculty and administrative positions may be "generated" by such formulas, sometimes to fractions of positions. Emphasis is upon "inputs" and "outputs" of the educational process, and students often become nameless "data" on a computer printout. Such terms as "student data course file," "cost estimation model," "faculty activity analysis," "student flow model," and "resource requirements prediction models" have become part of a new language of university administrators and state planners. The National Center for Higher Education Management Systems (NCHEMS) at the Western Interstate Commission on Higher Education in Denver has provided leadership to hundreds of institutions regarding new planning and management practices. In its publication *The Outputs of Higher Education* (1970), it is argued that our need to be responsive to society and to the individual will demand that higher education review its objectives and priorities. The best way to understand the values of an institution is to identify its priorities in its allocation of resources. The various activities and outputs of higher education need careful analysis if resources are to be allocated wisely.

A whole new group of specialists in management systems, planning, and "analysis" have appeared on the campus and in the state boards of higher education. Often, their role in policymaking, institutional planning, and even educational reform is as significant as that of the faculty.

Within this important development in higher education, students can easily be viewed merely as consumers, or as participants in an impersonal, prepackaged, well-managed, mechanical process. With the emphasis upon funding by total "credit hours produced," there is affirmation by implication that education is simply the accumulation of credits, and that other concerns and programs the institution may want to pursue are secondary, or no longer possible. Efficiency in the "management of education" may make good newspaper copy, but if it becomes the primary means used to evaluate an educational program, then the academic integrity of the institution can be compromised. Administrators and faculty are very busy people, and with the enormous complexity now involved in governing an institution, one ironic result of efforts to make institutions "more efficient" with new "management systems" may be to decrease their effectiveness due to the introduction of more bureaucracy, an avalanche of computer printouts, a staggering number of reports to file each month, and an increased emphasis upon impersonal, content-oriented course work.

Stephen Bailey (1973) has recently warned us about the "efficiency cultists":

By at least 1984, if we work hard we can make education supremely efficient and accountable . . . but there are limits to accountability, limits to efficiency, limits to slide-rule definitions of educational productivity. Surely the ultimate philistinism of our culture would be totally to impose management science upon the educational process.

Of course, there has been some poor management in higher education, as within all social institutions. Faculty and administrators have not always given clear definitions and stated specific objectives for the academic programs that have existed; and some, as a result, have become difficult to defend both on and off campus. Institutional officers have not been sufficiently aware of the differential costs of various academic programs at various levels, and they have not had as much reliable information available as is desirable in their planning efforts. The development of new management techniques, the quick availability of reliable information about costs of various programs, and the hard-headed evaluation of the "outputs" of higher education can be very beneficial in efforts to reform undergraduate programs.

The use of computers in educational planning and evaluation and the presence of program budgeting do not exclude the possibility of developing innovative and personalized academic programs for undergraduates. These relatively new (to the campus) techniques can be made to fit the educational structure and goals of the institution, although some persons may feel that the opposite is true. Developing written educational objectives for academic experiences and evaluating their impacts on students can result in more coherent and effective undergraduate programs.

Increasing Diversity of Students

The staggering increase in the number of students attending colleges and universities during the past fifteen years has been coupled with the appearance of much more heterogeneous student bodies. Open admissions and large numbers of new institutions have moved many colleges and universities beyond access on the basis of demonstrated academic merit into access without regard to past academic performance. Patricia Cross (1971) has studied the "new students" of the 1970s and has found them to be the offspring of blue-collar workers and to have had undistinguished academic records in the school system. They are less affluent than the more traditional students, and going to college is a new experience for them and their families. Many of them have completed high school with some difficulty, and they enter the college with academic limitations and different perspectives on life and learning than those of traditional college students.

Many traditional college programs and faculty are not well prepared for these "new students to higher education." New sensitivities have to be created to these students, and a careful assessment of the various academic programs should be made. In her book *Beyond the Open Door* (1972), Cross warns that it is unwise for institutions to try to make the "new students" into the image of traditional students. She argues that traditional methods with them may fail.

If higher education is going to serve these new students well, and develop programs that meet their needs, significant readjustment in attitudes and teaching objectives must take place. Too often, faculty may privately have some contempt for the "inferior" values and "disadvantaged" backgrounds of some students and, by their efforts and actions, inadvertently attempt to "make these new students over" into traditional, middle-class undergraduates. Indeed, too many programs in recent years with these "new students" have been geared to "correct the deficiencies" and overcome their "deprived backgrounds." More attention needs to be given to ways in which colleges can capitalize on the strengths of the "new students." This is a difficult task, because institutions will have to do a careful (and perhaps painful) analysis of how well they are prepared to meet these students' needs.

Many of our traditional undergraduate academic programs have not reflected an overall philosophical objective; they have lacked coherence. The addition of the large number of "new students" to higher education places an even greater obligation on faculty to develop new approaches to undergraduate education.

Many students today are not as closely related to their campuses as when most students attended traditional residential colleges and universities. The more typical college student in 1975 arrives daily to the campus by car, and leaves when his classes or "campus business" is completed. Often, these students are employed in the community, and especially at community colleges the students are likely to live at home with their parents. The sense of "being a student" is not as all-pervasive as it has been for more traditional students on residential campuses. The resulting impact of this situation is a lesser feeling of identity with the campus, a more impersonal, consumer-based relationship with the faculty, and less involvement in the day-to-day affairs of the institution on the part of students. The "school spirit" and sense of community that so many traditional residential campuses have become accustomed to are much more difficult to create. Moreover, the number of students transferring from one institution to another during their undergraduate programs (especially from two-year to four-year schools) increases each year, and this fact makes it more difficult to establish identity on a campus.

Many students now "stop out" of institutions, work or travel awhile, and then "pick up" their academic program again. Thus, the "student body," as it has been defined in previous years on more traditional campuses, is not a fixed or easily predictable group. It is a changing and diverse set of individuals who really follow no particular pattern at all. Another aspect of this diversity in students today is the more frequent enrollment of persons outside the traditional 18- to 22-year-old age group. Many campuses encourage the enrollment of older persons seeking second careers, persons who may begin college at age 28, women who decide to return to college to complete degrees begun ten years earlier, and other adult and even senior members of the community who can "benefit from the educational experience." The college experience is thus extremely complex, and it has significantly different meanings to various students. Despite this growing diversity among students in American higher education, many campuses still have not made significant adjustments in their educational programs; they have assumed, almost ostrichlike, that its students are still in the traditional world. Kenneth Keniston (1966) argues that it is essential for a campus to attempt to understand its students if it desires to have a substantial impact upon them. The interactions among the students themselves are very important, and the educational process extends beyond classroom instruction.

Despite some easing of external restraints in the past few years (e.g., the military draft), many students still feel that, in order to succeed in higher education, one must decide early on a professional future and then not deviate from this chosen path. The state of the economy, the comparative shortage of jobs, and the restrictive aspect of many undergraduate curricula operate to reinforce this perception by students. There is now a great deal of pressure on young people to make decisions about their academic and professional futures at an early age. Students are urged to select a "top-notch" college so that they might increase their chances of being selected for a prestigious graduate school. Few students have the important opportunity in undergraduate school to relax and experiment with their learning, because so many of them are caught up in the rush for competence. This pressure is a significant frustration for many students; yet most institutions do little to assist their students with this dilemma.

The increasing emphasis upon "career education," while perhaps serving the immediate needs of some students, too often ignores the need to consider the value implications of education. Students inevitably conclude that the institution does not care about the "value" of its educational program. McGrath (1974) argues that this lack of concern is an educational "time-bomb" for our society. He hopes that students will acquire a sense of the beautiful and of the morally good while in college but insists that continued emphasis upon specialized knowledge is incompatible with such a goal.

As the country continues to move from mass higher education to universal-access higher education, both the problems and the opportunities created are many. Institutions must carefully assess the nature of their students, and determine the kinds of educational programs they are best suited to offer. The Carnegie Commission report entitled *New Students and New Places* (1971) argues that it is time to look carefully at the nature of each of our institutions, and to examine the manner in which we use our resources to accomplish our objectives.

Summary

Higher education in the United States has experienced a tremendous expansion during the past fifteen years. This expansion has been coupled with a great increase in the number of institutions, especially community colleges, a movement in the direction from mass higher education to universal-access higher education, and considerable turmoil among students, faculty, boards of trustees, and legislators about the proper role for these institutions. At the same time that these dramatic developments have been taking place, there has been a great deal of confusion about the purposes of undergraduate educational programs, and many of these programs now lack coherence and commitment. There is a current mood for reform, but there are many factors that hinder institutions of higher education in the implementation of their reform efforts. Such factors as size, the decline of general education, the emphasis upon graduate programs, collective bargaining, soaring financial costs, and the increasing diversity of students have major influences upon undergraduate education. There is a disturbing absence of any emphasis upon the value implications of undergraduate education, and institutions now have a mandate to assess their own purposes, goals, students, and resources so that more effective undergraduate programs can be developed.

References

Ashby, Eric. *Any Person, Any Study*. New York: McGraw-Hill, 1971, p. 34. Reprinted with permission.

Bailey, Stephen K. "Combating the Efficiency Cultists." *Change Magazine*. June 1973, p. 8. Reprinted with permission.

Bell, Daniel. *The Reforming of General Education*. New York: Anchor Books, 1966, p. xxiii.

Berelson, Bernard, and Steiner, Gary A. *Human Behavior: An Inventory of Scientific Findings*. New York: Harcourt, Brace and World, 1964, p. 371.

Carnegie Commission on Higher Education. *New Students and New Places*. New York: McGraw-Hill, 1971, p. 9.

24

_____. *The More Effective Use of Resources*. New York: McGraw-Hill, 1972.

_____. *Priorities for Action*. New York: McGraw-Hill, 1973a, p. 54.

_____. *Governance of Higher Education*. New York: McGraw-Hill, 1973b, p. 44.

CBS News. "Higher Education: Who Needs It?"

Cross, K.P. "New Students of the '70s." *The Research Reporter*. Vol. 6, no. 4, 1971.

_____. *Beyond the Open Door*. San Francisco: Jossey-Bass, 1972.

Educational Testing Service. *Institutional Functioning Inventory*. Princeton, N.J., 1972.

Elman, Jeffrey. "Democracy, Students, and the University." In *Students and Society*. Center for the Study of Democratic Institutions. Santa Barbara, Calif., 1967, p. 15.

Feldman, K.A., and Newcomb, T.M. *The Impact of College on Students*. San Francisco: Jossey-Bass, 1969.

Hannah, John A. "The University as a Matrix." Address at the Conference on the Cluster College Concept, Claremont, Calif., March 30, 1967.

Heywood, Stanley. Quoted in Hodgkinson, *Institutions in Transition*. New York: McGraw-Hill, 1971, p. 228.

Hodgkinson, H.L. *Institutions in Transition*. New York: McGraw-Hill, 1971.

Keniston, Kenneth. "Faces in the Lecture Room." In Morison, Robert S., *The Contemporary University: U.S.A*. Boston: Houghton Mifflin, 1966, p. 322.

Kerr, Clark. *The Uses of the University*. Cambridge: Harvard University Press, 1963, p. 42.

Kunen, James S. *The Strawberry Statement: Notes of a College Revolutionary*. NewYork: Random House, 1968, p. 121.

Ladd, E.C., and Lipset, S.M. "Unionizing the Professoriate." *Change Reports*. 1973, p. 7.

Martin, W.B. *Alternatives to Irrelevance*. Nashville, Tenn.: Abingdon Press, 1968, p. 32.

McGrath, Earl. "The Time Bomb of Technocratic Education." *Change Magazine*. September 1974, p. 29.

Western Interstate Commission on Higher Education. *The Outputs of Higher Education*. Boulder, Colorado. 1970.

Wilson, Woodrow. "The Spirit of Learning." *Selected Literary and Political Papers and Addresses of Woodrow Wilson*. New York: Grosset and Dunlap, 1925, p. 244.

2 Whose Goals for Undergraduate Education?

In 1646, there was little doubt about the purposes of a college education. Each student was expected to be able to read Latin and Greek even before being admitted. The main purpose of the studies pursued by the students was to know God and Jesus Christ. Logic, natural and moral philosophy, arithmetic, geometry, and astronomy were the main subjects studied, and there were long and tedious lists of rules of conduct to follow.

There were very few students, of course, and the college was a homogeneous institution that trained a large number of its students for the clergy. One curriculum fit the needs of all the students, and "flexibility" in the educational program was really unnecessary. Moreover, the founders of Harvard did not distinguish sharply between secular and theological learning. They believed that a minister's education should be the same as an educated layperson's.

As the colonies grew, and as the small nation developed, the colleges changed. The American Revolution, of course, transformed thinking on almost all matters, and the new legal independence of the states presented new opportunities for higher education. The colleges of the colonial period were small and limited, and there was a desire to expand them into centers of more advanced study. Early state universities, such as Virginia, Georgia, and Michigan, were founded, and they aspired to rescue the collegiate system from sectarianism. Despite these efforts, the traditional college curriculum remained dominant through the first half of the nineteenth century. The Yale Report of 1828 was the most influential document in American higher education during that time, and this classic statement, written by Jeremiah Day and James Kingsley, quieted the critics of the college and the exponents of vocational and practical studies. It entrenched the classics at Yale for the rest of the century, and slowed the rate of curricular change and expansion. The Yale Report rejected the notion that the colleges must reform themselves and adapt to the new business character of the nation. It argued for a strong foundation in intellectual culture and a strict discipline of the mind. It reaffirmed the commitment to classical studies and the emphasis upon liberal knowledge. A student well versed in these traditional studies possessed the proper mental faculties to lead a rich and full life.

But the critics and reformers could not be silenced for long. The early nineteenth-century experience of various American educators at the German universities enhanced the American idea of what colleges could be. George Ticknor at Harvard proposed the division of the college into specialized departments in which related studies would be properly grouped. But he was a reformer ahead of his time, and after the substance of his proposals had been rejected, he resigned in 1836 (Hofstadter and Smith, 1961). The seeds of discontent with the current narrow collegiate purposes had been sewn, however, and they led to the American university movement.

Francis Wayland at Brown, Henry P. Tappan at the University of Michigan, and Andrew White at Cornell gave primarily leadership to the university movement in America during this period, and when the Morrill Act was passed in 1862, it was clear that American higher education was in the dawn of a new era.

The Morrill Act provided for the support and maintenance of at least one college in each state, where the leading purpose was to teach agriculture and the mechanic arts. While other scientific and even classical studies were not to be excluded, the emphasis was clearly on practical matters. Military tactics were also to be included in the curriculum.

The classical American college would never be the same again. At the Connecticut Agricultural College in 1884 the commencement exercises were graced by student addresses on "Irrigation and Drainage" and "The Feet of the Horse and Ox, and Their Diseases." Vocational and technical education had become a legitimate function of American higher education, and everywhere the idea of going to college was being liberated from the classic-bound traditions which for so long had defined the American collegiate experience (Rudolph, 1965).

It was entirely logical that the development of the elective system should emerge during the movement. When Charles William Eliot at Harvard expounded on the elective principle, he was attempting to transform a college with one uniform curriculum into a university without any prescribed course of study at all. He wanted to give Harvard students freedom of choice in their studies, and an opportunity to achieve depth in one subject. He was firm in his commitment to the idea that freedom of choice for students would help them become more responsible in their own academic habits. This elective principle was the instrument that built strong departments of knowledge and created the American university. Of course, the elective system had its critics, who claimed that it robbed the undergraduate curriculum of any logic and coherence, and that it granted too much freedom to young and inexperienced students. Others added that it eliminated a concern for the values and humanistic nature of education and emphasized in their place an exaggerated concern for practical, vocational, and narrow studies. Despite its detractors, it flourished, and institutions across the United States adopted it as they strove to serve the expanding needs of students and the nation. It was now an agency of social and economic mobility.

At the University of Chicago, where William Rainey Harper transformed Rockefeller's millions into a distinguished university almost overnight, the expectations and aspirations for the university movement were raised dramatically. Scholarship and departmentalism were emphasized strongly, and graduate education and research were for the first time given a prominent role in the university. Teaching was deemphasized, not so much consciously as it naturally declined into a role secondary to research and scholarship. As the university flourished, it became devoted to the discovery and promulgation of the truth, and academic freedom was necessary for universities to pursue this truth. The American Association of University Professors responded to this need in 1915 with the publication of their "General Declaration of Principles" (Hofstadter and Smith, 1961). The statement argued the case for freedom in the classroom for professors. For knowledge and understanding to advance, controversial issues had to be faced and probed, and widely divergent opinions discussed. While the individual professor was not under any obligation to hide his/her own opinion, it was his/her responsibility to introduce students fairly to the full range of competent thought on academic matters. The professor's task was not to give students easy conclusions on difficult issues, but to train them to think for themselves. With these principles in mind, students could have access to a full range of educational materials and could learn to make independent and intelligent decisions on their own. Although World War I was to have a major impact upon the development of academic freedom (for example, at Columbia), it became a necessary instrument for the advancement of scholarship, the development of the sciences, and the expansion of universities.

Predictably, the rapid growth and success of the university movement created an entire literature of discontent, and the growing numbers of students, new institutions, and rising expectations compounded the situation. Among such diversity, what should be the purpose of American higher education? Undergraduate education was viewed by Flexner as a "beehive of triviality and vocationalism," little more than a "service station" for the general public (Hofstadter and Smith, 1961). Robert Hutchins became the most influential proponent of classical, liberal education, and at the University of Chicago he attempted to correct the "great confusion" that had beset the higher education scene. If Hutchins's dramatic and controversial reforms in Chicago did not persuade the majority of institutions in America to achieve coherence in their undergraduate programs, they did reflect a movement toward general education. Meiklejohn at

Wisconsin, the faculty of Columbia College, and James Bryant Conant at Harvard were to give new meanings to liberal education and its role within the new American university.

In the Harvard Report on General Education (Conant, 1945), it was argued that specialism is the means of advancement for our social system. However, the report emphasized that a society that is composed of specialists is not an enlightened one, and the university must attempt to provide an effective general education for its students, while not turning its back on specialism. Value judgments need to be made by students in their academic pursuits, and the educational program must introduce students to the great ideas that have influenced our lives so greatly.

Although the Harvard Report on General Education had considerable influence, the postwar explosion of students and new institutions continued the rapid expansion of specialization, graduate departments, and federally sponsored research. Undergraduate education became, at many institutions, second in priority and prestige. The major research university was too preoccupied with money, public service, and research grants to worry much about undergraduate education. The curriculum, in the words of Warren Bryan Martin (1974), was "chicken wire and rough plaster—a flimsy house of intellect about which the correct question is not whether it now has coherence and integrity but whether it ever had any." The emergence of the community colleges and the development of the "multiversity" have further contributed to the current confusion over goals for undergraduate education. The American Council on Education saw this situation clearly in 1968, and dedicated its annual meeting to the topic "Whose Goals for American Higher Education?" (American Council on Education, 1968). The massive six-year study, undertaken by the Carnegie Commission on Higher Education, has largely been an attempt to give direction to higher education in assessing its current structure and purposes, and to stimulate reform and innovation within institutions. The next few years will attest to the effectiveness of the Commission's work.

There appears to be a growing realization on the part of many institutions that their goals need clarification and definition if they are to serve the needs of their students most effectively.

The Educational Testing Service has developed an instrument designed to assist institutions in identifying the major outcome goals that various groups have for their educational program. This instrument, the Institutional Goals Inventory (Peterson, 1972), includes the following outcome goals:

1. Academic development
2. Intellectual orientation
3. Individual personal development

4. Humanism/altruism
5. Cultural/aesthetic awareness
6. Traditional religiousness
7. Vocational preparation
8. Advanced training
9. Research
10. Meeting local needs
11. Public service
12. Social egalitarianism
13. Social criticism/activism

The Institutional Goals Inventory (IGI) has been used on several campuses and in state systems, and it has revealed some interesting and useful information. In California, in 1972, the IGI was administered to 116 institutions, and groups of faculty, undergraduates, administrators, regents, and community were compared on their goal priorities at the University of California, the state university and colleges, the community colleges, and private institutions. Research and advanced training were viewed as the highest-ranking current goals at the University of California by faculty, students, administrators, regents, and people of the community. However, most of these groups, especially the undergraduates, felt that there should be much greater emphasis upon individual personal development. The one exception was the faculty, whose first priority "should be" goal was intellectual orientation. Even at the community colleges, students felt that individual personal development should be a top-priority goal, but perceived that it was not. Most groups felt that such goals as humanism and cultural/aesthetic awareness should be stressed more by institutions than they currently were. Perhaps the most striking aspect of this study was the lack of satisfaction expressed about the ideal place of individual personal development on the one hand, and advanced training and research on the other. Evidently at many institutions, both students and faculty would prefer to emphasize a more personal approach to education, and lessen the importance of traditional research. There seemed to be less conflict among groups than there was general dissatisfaction with the overall current situation concerning goals. If these results can be viewed as reliable, there is clearly a mood for reform on the campuses. Many institutions could capitalize on this opportunity to define their mission, and in the process, give sharper focus to their undergraduate educational programs.

Edward Gross and Paul Grambsch studied university goals at 68 universities in the 1960s and sampled over 15,000 university faculty and staff in the process. They concluded that American universities emphasize the faculty's academic freedom, concern themselves primarily with goals relating to pure research and with maintaining or enhancing the university's position, and manifest relatively little interest in students beyond developing their scholarly abilities (Gross and Grambsch, 1968).

No argument is being made here for institutions to abandon their commitment to academic and intellectual achievement; however, there are many other goals and purposes that an institution might also consider carefully in its total program if it intends to have a positive impact upon its students. Some multipurpose institutions may attempt to serve all thirteen of the output goals in the Institutional Goals Inventory. It is a rare institution, however, that can effectively emphasize vocational preparation, research, social criticism, humanism, and academic development all at the same time! Too many institutions, in their desire to serve the needs of everyone, want to perform all these functions, and, in the process, create a good deal of confusion among students, faculty, and the public as to exactly what their primary role is. Students, institutions, and education itself can benefit if a campus would carefully assess its unique strengths and abilities, so that it might then focus its primary energies on a specific outcome goal. This is a difficult process, for it demands that an institution admit that it cannot do all things at once and that perhaps other campuses can serve education more effectively in some particular area. Some institutions may be very effective in encouraging their students to become active social critics, and may accomplish this goal through a strong commitment to individual personal development in a humanistic/altruistic manner. Others, by reason of tradition, types of students, background of the faculty, or expectations of the board, may not be inclined or capable in this area, and they may see their role as vocational preparation and meeting local needs. Too many institutions, regardless of their abilities, resources, and personnel, are striving to emulate the "prestige" goals of the "best" schools—research, advanced training, and academic development. In the process, they not only fail to achieve their aspirations, but actually work at crosspurposes to the educational goals they are best suited to serve. There must be a willingness on the part of academic institutions to commit themselves to realistic goals that they can achieve, as well as a recognition that such goals as public service, meeting local needs, individual personal development, and vocational preparation have just as much legitimacy and worth as research, advanced training, and academic development.

During the rapid expansion and specialization of higher education, there has been a decreasing willingness on the part of institutions to confront the area of students' values and the value implications of higher education itself. The increasing diversity among students, the elimination of the *in loco parentis* relationship of colleges toward their students, and the 18-year-old age of majority laws have encouraged institutions to divorce themselves from the lives of their students. However, the increasing depersonalization of higher education, the negative reactions of many students to their college academic experiences, and the Watergate scandal have caused some institutions to reexamine their role in this area. The view that it is sophisticated to consider all human behavior as being valuefree is being questioned more today. There seems to be a recognition among many educators that a "valuefree" view is unwise.

No social institution can assume responsibility for the personal actions of its graduates for all time, of course; but to pretend, while its students are there, that there is a dichotomy between fact and value is misleading, and, moreover, is poor education. Perhaps the most important step in learning decision making skills is to understand and clarify one's own values. "Valuefree" instruction does not really exist, and students most likely will not learn on their own how to apply the critical thinking they have been taught in lectures on academic subjects to social, political, and personal issues. The very selection of subject matter implies value judgments. Intellectual impartiality is clearly a value position itself regarding educa-tion, and if an institution engages in activity that may be viewed as con-tradictory to that value, students and others may conclude that the institu-tion's values are more attuned to money, research, and prestige than to intellectual honesty. The temptation for students and the institution to take refuge in a particular specialization away from value considerations is considerable, but it ignores the fact that ideas, courses, and research have consequences that need to be thought about seriously. In the late 1940s, the faculty at Amherst College devised a new curriculum that was deeply concerned with the problems of American democracy. The new edu-cational goal of the program was to teach students the consequences of their actions. In reviewing this goal in light of the Watergate affair, Hechinger (1974) argued that if this idea's time had come a bit earlier, it might have prevented a good deal of embarrassment, and even a few indictments: In the very goals that an institution emphasizes, it is stating its basic value commitments quite clearly.

There are many value implications in the process of higher education itself, and students' awareness of these values can enhance their involve-ment in their own education, and perhaps produce more effective and responsible graduates. When an institution invites students to participate on university councils and committees as voting members, it is committing itself to various values with its students. It is saying that individuals and their ideas have worth, that they should be listened to, that governance should be participating in nature, that decisions made in an atmosphere of open discussion are likely to be better than those made in secrecy, that participation implies an obligation on the part of students to learn all they can about the issues being discussed, that there are consequences for the various decisions these groups might make, and that students must thus assume part of the responsibility for the decisions. Each of these is a value position subject to considerable debate, and certainly not fixed or well known in the minds of all undergraduates.

Most institutions value very highly the right of each individual to decide her or his own point of view on intellectual, social, political, and religious issues. When persons or groups attempt to indoctrinate or impose their view on students, most institutions insist that not only is this inappropriate and poor educational methodology, but that it is also unethical. The institution places a high value on its respect for the individual and a negative value on methods that contradict this position. Institutions of higher education also place a high value upon the right of individual expression, and defend this right vigorously when it is threatened. When William Shockley was forced off the speaker's platform by the loud protests of persons on campuses who feel his views "do not deserve to be heard," there was widespread opposition to these actions, becasue most institutions place a high value on the right of individuals to express their views, and on the right of others to listen.

Most colleges and universities, as institutions, have not advocated political positions on various issues because they have always placed a high value on their role as objective and open organizations, where truth can be pursued in an impartial manner. The search for truth is valued highly, and in order to pursue this value, the institution must not align itself with any particular point of view politically, for then its search might not be impartial and its findings could be very subject to question.

Educational institutions also value intellectual honesty, as it is essential for the advancement of knowledge and for an accurate and reliable understanding of knowledge itself. In writing, research, and scientific experimentation, to misrepresent the results of data is not only inappropriate ethically, but also contradictory of the very purposes of doing the work in the first place. It violates a fundamental value assumption in higher education—mutual trust for others and their findings—and destroys the essence of the educational process. To do research is to share one's failures and limitations, as well as one's successes and discoveries, because one's ideas and work have consequences, which imply responsibility. The researcher may also have to consider the ethical implications of her or his work, and the use to which it might be put. Although an institution may value the search for truth for its own sake, to pursue with its students the probable ethical consequences of their investigations may be a value that is of equal importance.

An institution that carefully restricts the academic and social behavior of its students with elaborate and highly formal sets of rules, regulations, and procedures places a relatively low value on invidual responsibility. It evidently believes that students are not capable of selecting their own courses, of determining their own dormitory rules, or of deciding how to spend their academic time. One value that many students may learn from this kind of institution is that individual students cannot be trusted to make significant decisions and must be regulated under carefully controlled conditions. Other institutions may take a radically different approach to their students, giving them a great deal of responsibility and freedom in their academic and social lives, because the institution considers individual freedom an essential condition for educational growth.

There are many other examples that could be cited to illustrate the value positions inherent in educational programs in higher education. The point is that all institutions transmit values to their students, even when they claim that they are engaged in "valuefree" education. Paul Dressel (1968) has argued that colleges themselves must clarify their own value positions so that students can develop more awareness and concern regarding the implications of value differences. Students should become aware of their own values and that there are important differences in values from one culture to another. Such differences must be well understood if students are to learn to interact effectively with others unlike themselves.

Whose goals, then, for undergraduate education? The current scene, as has been pointed out, has evolved progressively from the classics, the elective system, the university movement, the general education movement, and the multiversity. The great confusion and lack of coherence in much of undergraduate education today stand at odds with historical claims for distinctiveness and diversity within American higher education. Institutions, in their desire to serve the needs of so many people at so many educational levels, have too often given low priority to thoughtful undergraduate teaching and programs. Rather than reflecting any overall educational purpose or value orientation, too often students' academic programs represent only the number of credits for graduation or the narrow requirements for a specific field of concentration. No suggestion is being made here for a homogeneity of institutional goals for undergraduate education; quite the contrary, the need is now very great for institutions to define what their special mission is to be, and then to put their energies resources, and imaginations to work. Only then can a true diversity and distinctiveness within undergraduate education be developed. This needed reassessment and this reexamination of undergraduate education are essential, for too many institutions have found that in their desire to be all things to all people, they end up not doing any one thing very well.

Before specific suggestions are presented for various undergraduate programs, it will be helpful to describe the students themselves—their characteristics, motivations, and life experiences. Chapter 3 addresses this topic, and Chapter 4 focuses on the impact of institutional programs upon students.

References

American Council on Education. *Whose Goals For American Higher Education?* Washington, D.C.: American Council on Education, 1968.

Conant, James B. *General Education in a Free Society: Report of the Harvard Committee.* Cambridge, Mass.: Harvard University Press, 1945.

Dressel, Paul. "The Meaning of a College Education." *Journal of Higher Education.* December 1968, p. 435.

Gross, Edward, and Grambsch, Paul. *University Goals and Academic Power.* Washington, D.C.: A.C.E., 1968.

Hechinger, Fred M. "Whatever Became of Sin?" *Saturday Review World.* September 21, 1974, p. 49.

Hofstadter, Richard, and Smith, Wilson. *American Higher Education: A Documentary History*, 2 vols. Chicago: University of Chicago Press, 1961.

Martin, Warren B. "The Ethical Crisis in Education." *Change Magazine.* June 1974, p. 3.

Peterson, Richard E. *Institutional Goals Inventory.* Princeton, N.J.: Educational Testing Service, 1972.

Rudolph, Frederick. *The American College and University: A History.* New York: Vintage Books, 1965, p. 263.

3 Undergraduate Students

If quality programs in undergraduate education are to be developed, a careful assessment of the characteristics of students is essential. It only seems logical that research should be conducted on the institution's student body as it maintains, revises, or develops its curricular and extracurricular programs. However, most institutions do not have much more than cursory summaries of what their students are all about, and they rely almost entirely in their planning upon informal hunches, historical tradition, and, especially, on what they wish their students were. Distinguished faculty researchers, who in their own fields would not think of planning a project without a careful initial assessment of available data, develop curricular programs, degree requirements, course content, and teaching methods with almost no reliable research data about students. Too often, all students are assumed to be equally receptive to the same teaching styles, time schedules, and curricular content. The striking differences that exist among students are not recognized in the planning process, and as a result, too often undergraduate programs may represent the needs of the faculty rather than those of the students.

It is important for institutions to know who their students are—their social and educational backgrounds, aspirations, attitudes and values, perceptions of the institution and its climate for learning, their living styles, their extracurricular preferences, and their learning styles. It is also important for a college or university to know how its students have changed, if at all, over a period of time regarding these matters, and to know if the students in its applicant pool actually represent the "types" of undergraduates being sought. If an institution makes substantial efforts in these areas, it can improve its educational planning, the selection of its faculty and staff, and the admissions process itself. There are, of course, very significant differences among students at various institutions, and reliable comparative data can be of real assistance to students, their parents, and school officials in the planning and selection process. Too often, stereotyped and inaccurate perceptions serve as the basis for student selection as well as for educational planning.

Quantitative assessments of students must be supplemented with qualitative, admittedly subjective, data about students. Undergraduates are not simply "unleavened lumps to be molded like ingots," by the educational process. Their personal and interpersonal experiences on the campus can

35

have a major impact upon the quality of their educational performance, and institutions who ignore such matters are not serving their students well.

The reluctance of institutions to study their own students as an essential part of their educational planning is especially ironic in 1975 because there is so much useful data available, and so many qualified persons and agencies are eager to supply it. To be sure, a "science of student ecology" has not yet emerged, but there are now more opportunities to obtain reliable data about students than in previous years.

This chapter purports to describe some of the current undergraduates in higher education, to comment on their experiences and attitudes as students, and to suggest various implications that these matters may have for undergraduate education.

Undergraduates: Who Are They?

As has been noted earlier, the national system of higher education is now moving from the provision of mass learning opportunities to universal access. The Carnegie Commission (1971) has noted this fact and suggested that the current enrollment of 8.5 million students will expand to 13.5 million by 1980, and to 17.4 million by the year 2000. It is important to mention, however, that the concept of "student" has already changed from previous years, and will continue to change in the future. "Students" have generally been largely thought to be persons between the ages of 18 and 22 who are engaged full time in academic pursuits. While this is still true of many undergraduates of course, there are now very large numbers of citizens who are only incidentally students—they also hold full-time jobs, they are older and are not necessarily interested in completing a degree, or they enter and "stop out" of the educational system as they please. Whereas part-time students were many years ago not so common, or in some cases actually discouraged or prohibited from attending certain colleges, they now comprise a major proportion of the total student population. In fact, some institutions now find such terms as "full-time-equivalent" and "part-time" student of little significance and no longer use them. This is particularly true at community colleges and at urban institutions. The vast numbers of citizens now enrolled and the even larger numbers predicted for the future must be understood in this new context. With so many options available now and in the future "students" are going to exhibit even more diversity in characteristics, learning styles, enrollment patterns, and educational goals. For institutions not to pay close attention to this unmistakable trend will not only impair their educational programs, but also may affect their ability to survive.

Given the tremendous diversity of undergraduate students in American higher education, it is impossible to describe them as a whole in a way that carries much meaning. Not only are there wide differences between students at various institutions regarding academic ability, motivation, socioeconomic background, race, sex, age, professional aspiration, and religious orientation, but there are also very significant variations within individual institutions. Thus it is sometimes hazardous to speak of all students, even at one college or university, as being of one type or background. A meaningful student profile at any institution will take careful note of these differences, and while it may reflect some overall trends and characteristics, its primary focus will be on the many subgroups that comprise the "student body."

The following descriptions of various "groups" of students, while obviously not exhaustive, is an indication of the diversity that exists among undergraduates.

Transfer Students

Undergraduates have moved from one institution to another for many years, but now with over 2 million students in community colleges, transfer students are no longer an "insignificant minority" on most four-year college campuses. Despite the striking increases in first-time matriculants in recent years, transfers to four-year institutions have increased at twice the rate of new first-year students (Sandeen and Goodale, 1971). Many institutions now award over one-half of their baccalaureate degrees to students who started college somewhere else, and there are now several new "upper-division" undergraduate institutions that enroll only juniors and seniors. Cross (1968) has shown that students who transfer to four-year colleges usually score lower on tests of academic ability than native students, and are likely to come from families of lower socioeconomic status than native students. Transfer students also tend to identify with their new institutions less than their native student classmates, which is, of course, understandable in terms of the shorter length of time they are enrolled there. But why focus specific attention on transfer students?

The experiences and attitudes of transfer students, at this point in higher education, are such that institutions need to take special note of them in their educational and extracurricular programs. Many transfer students feel that they are in an "educational no-man's-land," as they are either ignored or treated as second-class citizens by the institution. Too often, they are treated as first-year students or their special needs are not given any consideration in such areas as the availability of courses, student housing, financial aid, and academic advising. They are frequently "closed out" of many extracurricular activities, even though they might have been very involved at their previous institutions. Many transfer students feel that faculty both are not aware of, or overly concerned about, their previous academic work and do not know much about such institutions as community colleges. In the absence of workable and formally articulated agreements, previous academic work that transfer students have done may or may not be acceptable, depending upon the opinions of individual faculty members. Perhaps most difficult of all for transfer students at some colleges and universities, the faculty and administration may quietly resent the presence of transfers in large numbers, because these students may not fit the traditional stereotype these staff have for native students. All this has led Frederick Kintzer (1973) to label transfer students the "middlemen" in higher education.

These kinds of conditions on four-year campuses can lead to bitterness, resentment, and negative perceptions of the institution by transfer students. More importantly, they usually also result in less effective educational programs for these students, higher drop-out rates, and less institutional loyalty after graduation.

Not all transfer students, of course, have these kinds of experiences. However, they do represent a large and growing group of students, who may feel very alienated from the college and may not receive the optional educational benefit from the institution if it does not make special efforts to serve their academic, personal, and extracurricular needs.

Commuter Students

Most institutions now have large numbers of students who not only do not live on the campus, but who also drive or use public transportation from some distance to attend class. After their "campus business" is completed, they leave for home or job. This is not new, of course, and there are many institutions now where 100 percent of the enrolled students are commuters. Why, then, study commuter students, or single them out for any special attention?

Although there is considerable diversity among commuting students, the experiences of these students may differ considerably from students who live on or near the campus. Their access to academic programs, intramural sports activities, cultural events, the extracurriculum, and informal student-faculty relationships may be much less than that of on-campus students. Their feeling for a "campus community" may be almost nonexistent, and their identification with and knowledge of the campus may be minimal, through no fault of their own. Chickering (1974) has presented evidence that there are significant differences in the attitudes and perceptions between commuter students and on-campus students, and also that on-campus students are influenced more by the institution than are commuters. He has suggested that colleges interested in these findings should plan specific programs, such as temporary, short-term, on-campus living opportunities for these students. Commuter students usually have busy schedules off campus, and many institutions have found it difficult to achieve much success with some of the programs suggested here. Additional efforts and greater flexibility are needed in order to serve the educational and personal needs of these students.

International Students

A large number of four-year colleges and universities have enrolled substantial numbers of international students for many years. Indeed, many institutions have actively sought such students, and in their official publications they often boast of the "cosmopolitan" nature of their campus, where students from "50 different countries" (or more) are enrolled. Although the continuing enrollment of international students is happily no longer a very controversial issue, and although these students have made invaluable contributions to U.S. campuses, too often they have not been as well integrated into campus life as they could be, and, as a result, have not gained as much from or contributed as much to the educational process as they could. Although there are great differences among international students from African countries, the Middle East, and South America, the academic and extracurricular experiences of these students are too frequently isolated from the rest of the campus. Foreign-student advisors spend most of their time on mechanical problems, such as visas, housing, and financial aid, and institutions show very little appreciation of the substantial educational contributions these students have made and can make.

But why pay special attention to international students? Don't they simply want to get their specialized degrees and leave? There are tremendous educational opportunities that are presented to interested campuses that enroll substantial numbers of international students. Programs can be planned that benefit not only U.S. students and international students, but also the local community and its various organizations and schools. Many U.S. campuses now have the opportunity to "internationalize" the undergraduate experience for all interested students, if they would simply take the initiative. Where such efforts have been made for several years, such as at Iowa State University, greater understanding has resulted among all persons involved, and a new richness has been added to the educational program.

Black Students

It was not until the early 1960s that most predominantly white institutions "discovered" black students. Although most of them had enrolled black students for many years (except in the South), the presence of the new "black consciousness" was not really felt on these campuses until the 1960s. Blacks, of course, have been part of American higher education for a long time, as students at such institutions as Howard University, Morgan State, Florida A & M, Prairie View State, and Morehouse College. These colleges and universities have had many decades of experience in providing higher education for blacks; thus one should not be overly surprised to learn of the disdain felt when white institutions have announced "new" and "special" programs for black students! What has been labeled as an "innovation" for black students at a white university that has never worked very much with black students before, sounds very much like "standard operating procedure" for black institutions. Nevertheless, black students are enrolling at predominantly white four-year colleges and universities in large numbers, and these institutions need to learn a good deal about them and their experience at the institution if they are going to develop educational programs relevant to them.

One of the most unfortunate misconceptions that faculty and staff at predominantly white institutions have had about black students is that they are all somehow "disadvantaged." Besides being a very ethnocentric and disparaging term for any group of students, it simply is not true. Within the enrolled black student "group" at any institution is a wide range of socioeconomic and educational backgrounds. Despite the fact that this information seems perfectly logical, many faculty, administrators, and white students assume that black students must be poor or that they are from academically inferior high schools. They may also assume that "they're here only because the institution has to recruit them so it can retain its federal funds," and sometimes are genuinely surprised when they learn that not all blacks are enrolled in remedial or special programs. Of course, black students on white campuses are usually acutely aware of such perceptions, and this can have a major impact upon their experiences in the educational and extracurricular program.

Many campuses have noted that black students are among the most serious regarding their undergraduate studies, and also that a higher proportion of black undergraduates aspire to graduate and professional schools than whites (Bayer and Boruch, 1969). Many predominantly white campuses still seem to be experiencing the "two nations" syndrome, where there is little meaningful communication between white and black students (Centra, 1970). However, many campuses have made substantial efforts to create a more positive climate for good human relations, and it is encouraging to note the generally positive attitudes of undergraduates, both white and black, who are willing to work toward such improvements.

On many traditionally white campuses, sustained efforts need to be made to educate the faculty and the administration about black students and their diverse backgrounds and educational needs. More is needed, however, than just reliable information and data; programs need to be developed that encourage blacks and whites to work and play together, programs that involve both students and faculty. At the current time, most "communication" among blacks and whites on campuses is artificial, patronizing, and formal. If educational and extracurricular programs are going to be improved for both blacks and whites, these attitudinal barriers must be broken down. Frequently institutions either fail to recognize this situation or choose to ignore it. In doing so, they may avoid some unpleasant program failures, but they also are avoiding an important educational responsibility. Most college students are still quite flexible in their thinking and attitudes, and have a very healthy ability to confront difficult issues. Often, however, their formal educational curricular does not introduce them to the "real world" of human relationships. For black and white students, the college campus may represent the most ideal laboratory to learn about human relations. If institutions do not take an active role in providing leadership to their students on these issues, they are doing a real disservice to their undergraduates.

It is ironic that no one seems to be paying much attention to the role of the white student on the predominantly black campus. It is interesting to speculate on the reactions of some traditional educators when such white students are labeled as "disadvantaged" or "culturally deprived." Perhaps a carefully done study of white students at several black campuses would assist us in learning more about ourselves, our own ethnocentrism, and the need for educational programs that are adapted to meet the needs of all students.

Veterans

The "Vietnam era" veterans have enrolled in large numbers at institutions across the country. There are now over 1 million veterans enrolled in higher education. Some campuses may have more than 2,000 veterans as students. These undergraduates may test the flexibility of various academic requirements, as they attempt to get some form of credit for their previous academic experiences, both in and out of the military service. If their special needs are going to be met, careful attention needs to be paid to academic advising programs and student financial aid. Some veterans may have had uneven academic records three years ago, and since that time, they may have matured a great deal and also become more motivated. If the institution cannot exercise enough flexibility in its academic program (as in partial "forgiveness" provisions), then some of these students will enroll elsewhere. Although there are special federal financial aid programs for Vietnam veterans, there is less actual support for these students than there was for the World War II veterans. Many institutions have found that they need to serve in an advocacy role for their student veterans in their relationships with the federal government, so that existing financial aid programs can "deliver" on time.

Vietnam veterans have demonstrated a strong practical motivation in their academic programs. Many of them are older, of course, and have families, and they see the undergraduate degree primarily as a means to an economic end. At the same time that they are in a hurry to graduate, some of them have academic deficiencies which need special attention.

The Vietnam war was, of course, an extremely bitter experience for many Americans, and these veteran students harbor many of those residual attitudes. Many are cynical and highly skeptical about the sincerity of the government (or the educational institution), and some feel that they were used unfairly by their country only to return to an unappreciative and unsympathetic public. To ignore these attitudes or the special needs of these students simply reinforces the negative perceptions some Vietnam veteran students have at this time. The institution can serve both social and educational ends quite well as it works vigorously to know these students, and provide academic and extracurricular programs suited to their needs.

Women Students

The following statement, taken from one of the Carnegie Commission's reports (1973), reflects the changed social climate on campuses:

The second most fundamental revolution in the affairs of mankind on earth is now occurring. The first came when man settled down from hunting, fishing, herding, and gathering to sedentary agriculture and village life. The second is now occurring as women, no longer so concentrated on and sheltered for their child-bearing and child-rearing functions, are demanding equality of treatment in all aspects of life, are demanding a new sense of purpose.

We are rapidly moving toward a time where male and female students will enjoy the same access to all educational and extracurricular programs of the institution, and may aspire to and achieve professional roles in society on the basis of their demonstrated competence. However, there are still a number of problems facing institutions in this regard, and there are still barriers to women in higher education.

Although women comprise 50.4 percent of high school graduates nationally, they comprise only 43 percent of college graduates (Carnegie Commission, 1973). The percentage drops off even more dramatically (to 13.4) for doctoral degrees. These figures exist despite the fact that women students generally outperform men students, as measured by grades, in college. Obviously, there is a great deal of intellectual talent being lost to society as a result of cultural circumstances. Although there are few institutions that still overtly discriminate against women in undergraduate admissions, too often women are not made aware of or encouraged to pursue opportunities in certain areas of higher education. Once admitted, women students may experience considerable discomfort in some areas of the academic and extracurricular program of the institution, and may drift to less threatening and more traditional educational programs. Despite women's higher academic performance levels, the dropout rate is higher for women than for men (Carnegie Commission, 1973). Very few institutions provide attractive and realistic opportunities for women with children to return to their studies, and in most cases in our society women still are expected to assume the major child-care responsibilities. On some campuses where women students have organized efforts to improve their own opportunities for education through the provision of child-care programs, they have been met with severe obstacles, in the form of attitudes, policies, and money. Most often, women students have had to create child-care opportunities for themselves, apart from the institution. Many state institutions do not believe that the provision of facilities, staff, and programs in child care represent a "legitimate expenditure" of state funds, despite the fact that many of these same institutions may be offering "professional" training programs in their colleges of education in the area of early child development. Increasingly, the graduates of such programs may seek and find employment in child-care programs.

Although there are encouraging indications that women are entering some "traditionally male" fields in increasing numbers (especially law and medicine), there is still a strong need for special recruitment efforts. Simply to publish a brochure in an area such as mechanical engineering and pass it out to high school senior women is not adequate. Women need to be made personally aware, at an early age, of the opportunities and requirements for such a profession, and it must be demonstrated to them in real life situations how they can achieve their aspirations. Perhaps the most effective "evidence" for youth regarding their own aspirations is the presence of role models. As is well known, there are too few women serving as faculty members in an area such as mechanical engineering, and few, as well, practicing in the field. Substantial efforts need to be made to realize improvement in such areas. Once women students do enter such fields at the undergraduate level, the real and imagined pressures on them may be severe, and considerable courage and persistence may be needed to complete the academic program. Less than 10 percent of faculty members with the rank of full professor are women (Carnegie Commission, 1973), and there are even fewer women in major administrative positions in higher education. The affirmative action programs currently in operation may assist in effecting improvements in these areas, altbough financial pressures on institutions may greatly limit the employment market for all professors.

If institutions are going to meet the educational needs of their women students, they should develop effective programs in career planning and counseling. There are now very good opportunities for women in fields previously closed to them, and they need to be made aware of these options early in their academic careers. Aspiring to a particular profession, or changing one's major to an area that is relatively new for women, many times is more than just a mechanical process. It may be a decision that involves considerable emotional strain, anxiety, pressure from parents, and personal commitment. If the institution chooses to ignore such realities, blindly writing them off as *"in loco parentis* concerns of the past,"* it is missing an excellent opportunity to improve its educational programs for women. Professional academic and personal counseling programs, effectively presented to women undergraduates, not only can be of real assistance to those experiencing difficulties in their career and personal aspirations, but also can serve an an encouragement for other women students to explore new options.

The out-of-class climate at an institution may have a major impact on women students and on opportunities for them. If student life, in the form of student activities, publications, honoraries, and athletics, is dominated by men students (as is often the case), women students may not believe that there are options available to them to compete on equal terms in the campus "real world." Although the institution may not view the "extra-curriculum" as being important, it may be the major factor or set of circumstances that influences the aspirations and attitudes of students in the classroom. The faculty and administration are, on most campuses, really not part of the extracurriculum (by choice), but may exert major influences upon it by their attitudes, encouragement, and participation.

Although there is a revolution occurring within our culture regarding women—and this is reflected on the campuses among undergraduates—there may be significant socioeconomic and racial differences worth noting at various institutions. Quite often, the new options and life-styles pursued by women students are primarily those of middle-income and upper-income students. First-generation college women from lower socioeconomic backgrounds may have very different attitudes, feeling that college as is simply a method of getting a better-paying job and that things such as women's studies and "changing life-styles" are luxuries to be pursued by someone else. The academic and social experiences of black women undergraduates on predominantly white campuses have received very little attention, although there is evidence that they may have special needs (Centra, 1970). Some black women students may experience frustration in the limited social life available to them on campus, and many black women undergraduates may be reluctant to compete too aggressively with black male undergraduates. The combination of these factors may result in lack of enthusiasm for academic work, comparatively low academic and professional aspirations, and high dropout rates. The institution can well serve the needs of these students by paying special attention to these matters and by working jointly with them to improve their situation.

The "New" Students

Considerable attention has been focused recently on the "new" students in higher education, as especially noted in Cross's work (1972). Whereas most institutions of higher education have traditionally served students from middle- and upper-income levels, as well as students whose previous academic performance met traditional college-going expectations, this is no longer the case, as the country moves from mass to universal access to higher education.

The low academic achievers, who are gaining entrance through open admissions, comprise the dominant group among the "new" students. This new clientele for higher education consists of students who simply have not been part of higher education before, and the impact upon institutions may be very basic. Most institutions are ill-equipped to deal with these new students, and they present a major new challenge to higher education. Faced with large numbers of students who, by reason of past academic performance, are not well prepared for college work as it is presently defined, colleges and universities are having their academic flexibility tested as never before. Institutions that fail to make major adjustments in the curriculum and learning opportunities have discovered quickly that the "new" students "fail," drop out, or go elsewhere. Often institutions have emphasized the "deficiencies" of these students and have labeled them "high-risk"—a name that almost assures failure in itself. While most of the "new" students have performed poorly in high school, it is unlikely that these achievement patterns will change if the college or university uses the same methods to teach the same material.

Most institutions have been preoccupied for so long with imposing a fixed subject matter upon students, that the process itself has become almost sacred. Very little attention is paid to developing the talents and interests the "new" students bring to higher education. Colleges and universities do not have to lower their academic standards in order to work successfully with the "new" students. Cross (1973) has urged colleges to consider the notion that higher standards of performance need not mean higher levels of abstraction. She argues that colleges should begin with the students where they are at the time, and assist them in the development of their abilities. This can be done, she says, without merely duplicating the traditional academic model of past years.

Too much of the content of higher education has been taught to undergraduates with the (perhaps unconscious) implication that it is background for professional scholarship. Not many of the "new" students have much inclination to become professional scholars. These "new" students are attending institutions of higher education because of the rising educational aspirations of the citizenry. For the majority, the motivation for college does not arise from anticipation of interest in learning things in college but from the recognition that education is the way to a better job and a better life than those of their parents.

Some institutions, of course, are more adapted than others to adjust to these new students. Some are simply not willing to adjust. Clearly, however, institutions and their faculties will have to change as more and more of the "new" students are enrolled. In California already some 80 percent of the state's high school graduates continue their education (Cross, 1973). As this trend continues and spreads throughout the country, the impact upon institutions and their programs will be considerable.

The presence of large numbers of these "new" students will undoubtedly further the emphasis upon career education, and will enhance the role of the student as a "consumer." The traditional "collegiate" models of campus life just do not fit the styles of these students very well. Much of the campus extracurricular activity may seem unimportant to the "new" students, and new programs may need to be offered to attract them to out-of-class functions.

Perhaps most importantly, attitudes of faculty and others in higher education must change if these students are going to achieve success at the institution. Most of these "new" students have experienced years of comparatively low achievement in the school system already, and may have rather low opinions of themselves as potential learners. If they perceive that the institution views them as a "special experiment," or as second-class citizens, it is unlikely that they will realize much success or even gain from the experience. Many of these students have equated too much of their school experience with "failure," have have come to expect that it is almost inevitable for them. Many institutions have carefully restructured their programs for "disadvantaged" students, and have rethought their own values and objectives as they have become more sensitive to the human needs of these "new" students. Only through such efforts are the high dropout rates for these students going to be lowered and effective educational programs developed.

Preprofessional Students

There are limited numbers of spaces in the various professional schools in higher education, such as law, medicine, nursing, veterinary medicine, pharmacy, and dentistry. As interest has grown recently in these fields at an unprecedented rate, the competition among undergraduates for places in these professional fields has become stiff. The rapidly expanding opportunities for women and ethnic minorities, aided by affirmative action programs, have intensified the competition. Undergraduates with serious professional school aspirations begin their intense efforts to achieve a high grade point average immediately upon enrollment as first-year students, and some prepare for such exams as the Law School Admissions Test and the Medical College Admissions Test as if their very lives depended on their performance.

There is reason for undergraduates to be so competitive. The number of students applying to American medical schools rose from 18,724 in 1968 to about 40,000 in 1974, and the number of students taking the Law School Admiissions Test has almost tripled in the last six years (Howard, 1974).

There has always been a substantial proportion of new undergraduates who aspired to professional schools, but changed their minds, their majors, or their motivation during college. Others persisted, but were not admitted to any professional school. Now, however, the numbers are much larger, the competition much more intense, and the chances to get "shut out" of the system much greater.

The effect of this competition for places in professional schools can be traumatic to undergraduates themselves and upon their educational programs. They may become so preoccupied in a grim and frenetic way that the value of a "free-floating exploratory experience" is squeezed out. The almost inevitable apprehension about grades makes learning almost secondary to quality-point averages. They may not dare to experiment with course work that may not "look good" to professional schools, and they may graduate with the most narrow of academic programs. Some may even resort to unethical practices in their intense desire to be accepted, and, of course, the professions can only suffer from persons with such uncontrolled ambition, should they be admitted.

It is ironic that educators should express concern over the serious academic motivation of undergraduates. For generations, faculty have complained about the casual approach too many students took to their studies. But this concern that faculty and others have for these students is well founded. The "walking wounded" are many. Large numbers of students simply cannot be admitted to professional schools, despite their high motivation and aspirations. The need for careful, timely, and sensitive career and personal counseling for these students is crucial. A humane institution will not simply ignore its senior students who, after years of hard work, see their professional dreams come crashing down while very few other viable options are available to them.

The competition for places in professional schools is not going to diminish in the near future. Institutions can serve their undergraduates extremely well by recognizing the nature of the competition, the human considerations inevitably involved, and the importance of career and personal counseling for these undergraduates.

Transfer students, commuter students, international students, black students, veterans, women students, the "new" students, and preprofessional students represent only some of the diversity that exists within higher education. On most campuses, all these undergraduate groups are enrolled, along with many others. There are great differences among "student bodies" at various institutions. If a college or university is to develop an effective educational program that has a positive impact upon its undergraduates, it needs to be knowledgable about its students—their composition, attitudes, academic aspirations, and perceptions of the institution.

There are some excellent research instruments now available to institutions attempting to understand the nature of their students. Regular and planned use of these tools can provide reliable information to a college or university, which can prove essential to its educational planning and development. A few of these available methods are reviewed briefly here in an effort to indicate the kinds of data that can be provided about students, and how they can be used for effective educational planning.

Research Instruments Available

The Clark-Trow Model

Burton Clark and Martin Trow have developed a scheme for classifying students into four types, based upon the degree to which students are involved with ideas and the extent to which students identify with their college (Clark and Trow, 1966). Students are asked to read four statements, each of which describes a "personal philosophy" about what higher education should be. Then the student identifies the statement that comes closest to his or her own philosophy of higher education. The four types are called: (1) vocational, (2) academic, (3) collegiate, and (4) nonconformist. A description of each follows.

Vocational: This philosophy emphasizes education essentially as preparation for an occupational future. Social or purely intellectual phases of campus life are relatively less important, although certainly not ignored. Concern with extracurricular activities and college traditions is relatively small. Persons holding this philosophy are usually quite committed to particular fields of study and are in college primarily to obtain training for careers in their chosen fields.

Academic: This philosophy, while it does not ignore career preparation, assigns greatest importance to scholarly pursuit of knowledge and understanding wherever the pursuit may lead. This philosophy entails serious involvement in course work or independent study beyond the minimum required. Social life and organized extracurricular activities are relatively unimportant. Thus, while other aspects of college life are not to be forsaken, this philosophy attaches greatest importance to interest in ideas, pursuit of knowledge, and cultivation of the intellect.

Collegiate: This philosophy holds that besides occupational training and/or scholarly endeavor, an important part of college life exists outside the classroom, laboratory, and library. Extracurricular activities, living-group functions, athletics, social life, rewarding friendships, and loyalty to college traditions are important elements in one's college experience and necessary to the cultivation of the well-rounded person. Thus, while not excluding academic activities, this philosophy emphasizes the importance of the extracurricular side of college life.

Nonconformist: This is a philosophy held by the student who either consciously rejects commonly held value orientations in favor of her or his own, or has not really decided what is to be valued and is, in a sense, searching for meaning in life. There is often deep involvement with ideas and art forms both in the classroom and in sources (often highly original and individualistic) in the wider society. There is little interest in business or professional careers; in fact, there may be a definite rejection of this kind of aspiration. Many facets of the college—organized extracurricular activities, athletics, traditions, the college administration—are ignored or viewed with disdain. In short, this philosophy may emphasize individualistic interests and styles, concern for personal identity, and, often, contempt for many aspects of organized society (Educational Testing Service, 1965).

While this typology is not meant to describe individual students, it does yield valuable information about the general orientation of a total student body. Some campuses may have large numbers of students in the vocational subculture, for example; others may have a very small proportion. The same kinds of differences prevail in other subcultural categories as well. In addition, there usually are striking differences among students on the same campus when students are compared by curriculum, place of residence, or socioeconomic background. Not to take note of such differences may result in some poorly received educational programs.

Students in the vocational subculture are often found in urban and commuter institutions and are frequently attracted to courses of study that are highly practical and "no-nonsense." They have little time (or money) to waste in their pursuit of a better job. They fit the "consumer" notion of students who are in college to "buy their education as one buys groceries." They are usually not much involved in extracurricular activities, and are not much interested in academic work beyond what is required to pass each course. They are usually more attracted to lecture-type presentations in class, as opposed to open-ended discussions, and may have a very unenthusiastic response to any lack of structure in a professor's teaching methods. They also may not respond favorably to essay-type examinations, preferring instead objective and clearly defined evaluations. Most of the "new" students described by Cross (1972) fit this subcultural typology. There may be other important characteristics of these students worth noting which could aid in educational planning. Some small, highly selective liberal arts colleges may have as few as 5 percent of their students identifying with this vocational type, while a community college or an urban commuter institution may have as high as 75 percent of its students in this category.

Students in the academic subculture will be dominant on some campuses and marginal or almost invisible on others. Their emotional tie to the college is through the intellectual values of its serious faculty members. While they may be aware of their own career aspirations, their primary interest is in knowledge and learning for its own sake. Many faculty members, especially those who teach in such areas as the social and behavioral sciences and the humanities, would like to work with students who fit this description, but most often they do not. One of the real difficulties many colleges have had is that they have designed educational programs with the (hoped for) assumption that their students were strongly motivated in a pure academic sense. A few highly selective liberal arts colleges have a substantial proportion of their students in the academic category, but most institutions, especially the emerging state colleges, urban commuter schools, and the community colleges, have a very small proportion of these students in their student body.

As Richard Peterson (1965) notes, "the most widely held stereotype of college life pictures the collegiate subculture, a world of football, fraternities and sororities, dates, cars and drinking, and campus fun." While students in this category usually generate most of the loyalty and attachment to the college, they may be largely indifferent to the serious academic demands of the institution. It is comprised mostly of middle- and upper-income students, and this subculture flourishes on the residential campuses of large state universities. These students may view participation in extra-curricular activities as being as important as their classwork. Where the collegiate subculture dominates on a campus, it is doubtful that serious academic work can be sustained for very long. As increasing numbers of the "new" students enroll in higher education, the impact of this powerful student subculture on campus life will be diminished.

What Clark and Trow call the "nonconformist" subculture is usually the smallest group on most campuses, composed of those students who are primarily concerned with pursuing an identity, as opposed to a diploma, knowledge, or fun, as with the other three groups. These students are often involved with ideas, but they are not as oriented to the campus per se. Indeed, a good part of their strategy of independence and criticism may be based upon a detachment from the faculty, or a generalized hostility to the college. Even though their numbers may be comparatively small, their visibility and influence may be considerable on the campus.

Without any attempt to stereotype students into fixed categories, an institution can learn a great deal of valuable information about the general composition of its student body by using this Clark-Trow typology model. The campus profile varies greatly from one institution to another, and, as has been indicated, these matters may have an important influence on the success of various educational programs, and should be considered in the planning process.

The College and University Environment Scales (CUES)

This instrument, published by Educational Testing Service (1962, 1969), is designed to describe the institutional climate of a campus through the perceptions of its students. The CUES provides a measure of the environment along five dimensions, which reflect ways in which colleges differ from one another. These scales are described, briefly, as follows:

Practicality: To what extent does the campus atmosphere emphasize the concrete and realistic, rather than the abstract and speculative? A high score indicates that organization, system, and procedure are important, as

well as status and practical benefit. Also, order and supervision are characteristic, both of the administration and of the classwork.

Community: Is the environment cohesive and supportive? Do a concern
for group welfare and a feeling of group loyalty pervade the campus? High
scores indicate a supportive and sympathetic environment; low scores
suggest one where privacy is important and detachment prevalent.

Awareness: How much concern is there for self-understanding and identity? How much active interest is there in a wide range of esthetic forms?
How pronounced is personal involvement with the world's problems and
the human condition?

Propriety: Decorum, politeness, consideration, thoughtfulness, and caution are elements of this scale. A low score would indicate an atmosphere
that is relatively demonstrative and assertive, more impulsive than cautious, more free-wheeling than polite and mannerly.

Scholarship: This scale reflects interest in scholarship, in academic
achievement, and in competition for it. High scores indicate emphasis upon
intellectual speculation, interest in ideas as ideas and in the pursuit of
knowledge for its own sake (Educational Testing Service, 1966).
   This profile of the campus environment provided by the CUES can be a
valuable tool in understanding the climate for learning, and comparing, for
example, faculty and student perceptions. Moreover, the CUES can provide valuable insights to educational planners. For example, people on
many campuses may feel that their institution places an important priority
on involvement with the world's problems and the condition of human
beings. However, upon administering the CUES, they may discover (as
many have) that students do not feel this is a particular characteristic of the
institutional climate ("awareness" scale). Such information can then be
used effectively in planning for change. Many campuses have grown dramatically in size since the early 1960s, yet they still feel strongly about the
"friendly, informal, cohesive" nature of their campus. In fact, many of
them speak proudly of this with prospective students and their parents.
However, information provided on the "community" scale of the CUES
might change their perceptions. Students on many campuses of over 20,000
often have very different perceptions of the cohesiveness and personal
support aspects of the institution than do students on campuses of under

5,000. Often educators assume incorrectly that their own historically based perceptions still prevail and can be acted upon in new academic programs.

The CUES, while it does not describe individuals, does yield valuable data about institutional climate. Such information can assist institutions in program development and understanding, as well as prospective students and their parents in the admissions-selection process.

The Institutional Functioning Inventory (IFI)

This research tool was developed by the Educational Testing Service (1970) in response to the need for institutions to take stock of themselves and their strengths and weaknesses, as increasing numbers of people press the colleges for change. The IFI helps to show how faculty, students, administrators, and other constituent groups perceive the teaching practices, governance arrangements, administrative policies, types of programs, attitudes of groups of people, and other important aspects of campus life. Specifically, the IFI yields an analysis of the college in terms of the eleven dimensions defined briefly, as follows:

Intellectual-Aesthetic Extracurriculum (IAE): The extent to which activities and opportunities for intellectual and aesthetic stimulation are available outside the classroom.

Freedom (F): The extent of academic freedom for faculty and students as well as freedom in their personal lives for all individuals in the campus community.

Human Diversity (HD): The degree to which the faculty and student body are heterogeneous in their backgrounds and present attitudes.

Concern for Improvement of Society (IS): The desire among people at the institution to apply their knowledge and skills in solving social problems and prompting social change in America.

Concern for Undergraduate Learning (UL): The degree to which the college—in its structure, function, and professional commitment of faculty—emphasizes undergraduate teaching and learning.

Democratic Governance (DG): The extent to which individuals in the campus community who are directly affected by a decision have the opportunity to participate in making the decision.

Meeting Local Needs (MLN): Institutional emphasis on providing educational and cultural opportunities for all adults in the surrounding communities.

Self-study and Planning (SP): The importance college leaders attach to continuous long-range planning for the total institution, and to institutional research needed in formulating and revising plans.

Concern for Advancing Knowledge (AK): The degree to which the institution—in its structure, function, and professional commitment of faculty—emphasis research and scholarship aimed at extending the scope of human knowledge.

Concern for Innovation (CI): The strength of institutional commitment to experimentation with new ideas for educational practice.

Institutional Esprit (E): The level of morale and sense of shared purposes among faculty and administrators (Educational Testing Service, 1972).

The IFI can assist institutions in understanding how their students feel about the importance of undergraduate education (this may prove embarrassing!), the availability of intellectually and aesthetically stimulating activities outside the classroom, and the campus governance process itself. There usually are significant differences in the way in which students and faculty view the intellectual and aesthetic climate of the institution. From such information, useful deliberations, seminars, and planning efforts could begin to reach satisfactory goals.

A college that uses the IFI in a systematic manner, administering it at selected times over a period of years, can learn a great deal about actual changes that are occurring on its campus, and can likewise assess the relative impact of a number of changes it has made—for example, in its admissions policies, in its basic undergraduate program, or in its governance process. Such institutions should be better able to plan new programs and to respond to external and internal pressures in their efforts to serve their students effectively.

The College Student Questionnaire (CSQ)

This instrument was developed by the Educational Testing Service (1965) as a means of gathering diverse biographical and attitudinal information about college students. It consists of three main sections: (1) educational and vocational plans, (2) college activities, and (3) student attitudes. In addition, scores on eleven scales are obtained, and brief definitions of them as listed here:

Satisfaction with Faculty (SF): This refers to a general attitude of esteem for instructors and the characteristic manner of a student-faculty relationship at the respondent's college. Students with high scores regard their instructors as competent, fair, accessible, and interested in the problems of individual students. Low scores imply dissatisfaction with faculty and the general nature of student-faculty interaction.

Satisfaction with Administrators (SA): This is defined as a generally agreeable and uncritical attitude toward the college administration and administrative rules and regulations. High scores imply satisfaction with both the nature of administrative authority over student behavior and personal interactions with various facets of the administration. Low scores imply a critical, perhaps contemptuous, view of an administration that is variously held to be arbitrary, impersonal, and/or overly paternal.

Satisfaction with Major (SM): This refers to a generally positive attitude of respondents about their activities in their field of academic concentration. High scores suggest not only continued personal commitment to present major fields, but also satisfaction with the departmental procedures, the quality of instruction received, and the level of personal achievement within one's chosen field. Low scores suggest an attitude of uncertainty and disaffection about current major field work.

Satisfaction with Students (SS): This refers to an attitude of approval in relation to various characteristics of individuals comprising the total student body. High scores suggest satisfaction with the extent to which such qualities as scholastic integrity, political awareness, and particular styles and tastes are perceived to be characteristic of the student body. Low scores imply disapproval of certain characteristics that are attributed to the overall student body.

Study Habits (SH): This refers to a serious, disciplined, planned orientation toward customary academic obligations. High scores represent a perception of relatively extensive time devoted to study, use of systematic study routines and techniques, and a feeling of confidence in preparing for examinations and carrying out other assignments. Low scores suggest haphazard, perhaps minimal, attempts to carry through on instructional requirements.

Extracurricular Involvement (EI): This is defined as relatively extensive participation in organized extracurricular affairs. High scores denote support of and wide involvement in student government, athletics, religious groups, preprofessional clubs, and the like. Low scores represent disinterest in organized extracurricular activities.

Family Independence (FI): This refers to a generalized autonomy in relation to parents and parental family. Students with high scores tend to perceive themselves as coming from families that are not cloesly united and as not consulting with parents about important personal matters, as not concerned about living up to parental expectations, and the like. Low scores suggest "psychological" dependence on parents and family.

Peer Independence (PI): This refers to a generalized autonomy in relation to peers. Students with high scores tend not to be concerned about how their behavior appears to other students, not to consult with acquaintances about personal matters, and so on. They might be thought of as unsociable, introverted, or inner-directed. Low scores suggest conformity to prevailing peer norms, sociability, extraversion, or other directedness.

Liberalism (L): Liberalism is defined as a political-economic-social value dimension, the nucleus of which is sympathy either for an ideology of change or for an ideology of preservation. Students with high scores (liberals) support welfare statism, organized labor, abolition of capital punishment, and the like. Low scores (conservatism) indicate opposition to welfare legislation, tampering with the free enterprise system, to persons disaggreeing with American political institutions, etc.

Social Conscience (SC): Social conscience is defined as moral concern about perceiving social injustice and what might be called institutional wrongdoing (as in government, business, unions). High scorers express concern about poverty, illegitimacy, juvenile crime, materialism, unethical business and labor union practices, draft and government, and the like. Low scorers represent reported lack of concern, detachment, or apathy about these matters.

Cultural Sophistication (CS): This refers to an authentic sensibility to ideas and art forms, a sensibility that has developed through knowledge and experience. Students with high scores report interest in or pleasure from such things as wide reading, modern art, poetry, classical music, discussion of philosophies of history, and so forth. Low scorers indicate a lack of cultivated sensibility in the general area of the humanities (Educational Testing Service, 1965).

This instrument perhaps yields more specific information about students than any other currently available. Besides providing a highly useful set of scales, it offers almost unlimited opportunities to compare students from one institution to another, or to compare students within the institution regarding college major, place of residence, family background, age, or sex. There are two forms to the CSQ: one for entering students, the other for enrolled upperclass students. One of the most revealing exercises a college can undertake with this instrument is to administer it first to its entering first-year students and then to this same group two or three years later. The changes (or lack of them) in students over this time period can assist the institution in learning if its educational program is having the intended effects. Dramatic differences exist from one campus to another in terms of CSQ results on the eleven scales, yet corresponding differences in educational programs, teaching methods, and academic emphasis do not exist very often.

The American College Testing Program (1974) offers the "Class Profile Service," which provides a comprehensive description of an entering class. This profile includes information about students' academic abilities, goals, and aspirations; selected needs relevant to student personnel services; students' out-of-class accomplishments; and demographic characteristics of students. This material can be collected each year, and important changes and trends in the students enrolling in the institution can be noted. It can be of assistance in such areas as recruitment, admissions, instructional planning, and student counseling.

The *Survey of College Achievement* (Educational Testing Service, 1972) provides a measure of group achievement in the first two years of college. It can be used as a basis for comparisons of first-year students by subgroup as well as of growth of student groups along dimensions such as sex, aptitude, major field, or grade point average.

Finally, the *Omnibus Personality Inventory* (Heist and Yonge, 1962, 1968) is a useful instrument that assesses attitudes, values, and interests of students. It can provide helpful information about development and change among students.

As the diversity of students continues to increase in higher education, institutions should plan to assess their students carefully on an organized and periodic basis. The process is not overly complicated. There are a number of excellent research instruments available, and the results can go a long way in helping an institution plan more effective educational programs and understand its students more completely.

Attitudes of Students

Although many colleges and universities may not view student attitudes as crucial to the educational process (or even as any of their concern), they can have a major impact upon the learning climate of the institution and the relationship of the students to the college. Frederick Rudolph (1966) has argued that

the most sensitive barometer of what is going on at a college is the extracurriculum. It is the agency that identifies students' enthusiasm, their understanding of what a college should be, and their preferences. It reveals their attitude toward the course of study, and it records the demands of the curriculum, or the lack thereof.

To ignore the effect of such informal student interactions is to isolate the institution's academic program from the students and their lives. The separation of the curriculum and the extracurriculum is illustrated well in Robert Ward's (1974) statement about education at Amherst.

A friend of mine at a New York hospital recently told me of the possibility that science will be able to sever completely the human mind from the rest of the body and with appropriate tubing, machinery, and pumps, keep the brain alive indefinitely with no connection to the heart. My comment was that this was really not new—we had been doing it for years at Amherst.

If the student essentially perceives and lives two separate lives at the university—one in the classroom, the other outside of it—and does not see any logical connection between the two, then the institution's educational program has fallen very short of what it could be. This does not mean that professors have to leave their laboratories and become drinking companions with undergraduates. While few students seek professors as personal friends, the educational needs of undergraduates are well served by professors who know and care who the students are, how they live, and what their aspirations are. While reacting against *in loco parentis* during the

1960s, students were pleading to be treated as adults—they were not requesting to be ignored or to be treated as impersonal numbers. Most colleges that have studied their dropouts carefully have discovered that many more students leave for personal reasons than for reasons of academic failure. Often, students find the college experience impersonal, and so disconnected with their lives that they simply leave it for something else.

Most students come to college with a great deal of excitement and willingness to do the work demanded of them, but their expectations and performance usually decline very rapidly during the first few months of the first year (Kauffman, 1968). Frequently a reason is that the institution presents an ''educational program'' that the students view as something separate from themselves as people. Indeed, some students clearly prefer their education this way. They have learned to be quite comfortable in class, assured that they will never be called upon (especially by name!) to relate the material to themselves or the problems they face in their lives. An impersonal education can be ''safe'' for students and faculty; it can protect each of them from having to expose their innermost thoughts, values, and attitudes to others, and having these subjected to close scrutiny. It is also safe in that it lessens the probability of failure, of having one's ideas rebuked. It also can be very boring for students and faculty, and can lead them to go ''do their own thing''—almost anything—that seems to make sense for them. It is the kind of education that ignores the most perplexing educational issue of our day—how to assist the rank and file of students in reaching decisions on the complex social, political, and moral problems which they inevitably face.

There was a great deal written, of course, during the 1960s about students and the ''new attitudes'' they were bringing to the campuses. However, instead of leading the society, as some thought students were doing at the time, it is clear that student attitudes at any time are mainly a reflection of society's agenda. Yankelovich (1964) completed an exhaustive study of youth values and found that students have shifted their interests away from social issues and are now more concerned with themselves. The high-pitched emotional involvement that appeared to be so strong during the 1960s has been replaced with a concern for self-fulfillment and professional preparation. This shift to privatism on the part of students is troublesome if students see little value in pursuing educational issues outside of carrer planning. For an institution not to take note of these shifts in attitudes is potentially damaging to its educational program. It is not being suggested that colleges should adjust what they do to fit whatever the students want at the time—to do so would be foolish and without educational justification. A college, in noting current attitudes of students, may decide to develop programs which are designed to change student attitudes, not simply reinforce existing ones. If Yankelovich's data are correct, many institutions may have to exert more vigorous efforts than before in convincing their students to be concerned about the social, political, and moral needs of the world.

As American society increases in complexity, the period during which young people are "preparing for life" seems to grow longer and longer. This constant state of "always being potential" can be very frustrating and unrealistic for college students. This extended period of time between adolescence and adulthood has been labeled "the stage of youth" by Kenneth Keniston (1970)—a new stage of life, previously unrecognized. The central conscious issue during the "stage of youth" is the tension between self and society. The rule is pervasive ambivalence toward both self and society. Colleges can assist its students in this difficult period by providing effective services in counseling, career planning, and academic advising. It can also offer (perhaps require) "real world" experiences that place students in situations where they are not simply "preparing for the future," but are actual contributing members of society. The current interest in cooperative education programs reflects this need. Many students now are "stopping out" of college for a year or two, often to place themselves consciously in the "real world," so they can escape the "world of eternal preparation," as some of them view college.

The impersonal and unrealistic nature of much of undergraduate education can be viewed, at least partially, as a contributing factor to the increasing "privatism" of students. Given to believe that even education is devoid of much personal meaning for them, students may further disassociate themselves from others, and may be increasingly distrustful of any long-term personal relationships. This had led to the popularly expressed notion on campuses that "the only things I own are my own feelings." Seen in this context, the abuse of drugs (done mostly in private), the "rip-offs" of personal and public property, and the increasing impersonality in sexual relationships among young people are perhaps more understandable. Our educational programs are not serving students well if at graduation they are convinced that the most effective way to deal with an impersonal and troubled world is to be cautious, personally exploitive, distrustful of lasting relationships with others, and deliberately separated from the social, political, and moral needs of the world.

The attitudes that students develop as a result of their college experience can be a more powerful determinant of their later success than the content-oriented knowledge that they accumulate. Colleges and universities can have a major impact upon the lives of their students, but it requires careful planning and conscious, consistent efforts over a period of time. To "write off" student attitudes as a peripheral or frivolous concern, unrelated to the academic program of the institution, is not evidence of a sophisticated or mature "university"; furthermore, it is not what most students want. It is to wear academic blinders, which may prevent the institution from serving the real educational and human needs of its students.

Summary

Students, while increasing in numbers, are also increasing in diversity. As the nation moves from mass higher education to a universal-access system, "new" students are appearing on the campuses for whom many colleges are not well prepared. It is hazardous, among this tremendous diversity of students, to speak accurately or meaningfully about all students, even at one institution. The special needs and characteristics of such student "groups" as transfers, commuters, veterans, women, blacks, preprofessionals, and the academically ill-prepared are important to note as institutions strive to make their educational programs serve their students. Colleges and universities can also benefit from careful and periodic assessments of their students by using a variety of excellent research instruments currently available. There are striking differences between students on one campus and another on a wide array of measures, and also among students within one institution. Such reliable information can, over a period of time, assist colleges and universities learn more about their students, and aid them in their educational planning. Student attitudes, although they may change from one period of time to another, reflect the mores and values of the society. Instead of ignoring the attitudes of students as being irrelevant, colleges should make efforts to relate the academic program more effectively to the lives of their students and to the needs of society. The current mood of many young people seems to be focused on personal, career-oriented values, somewhat unconnected with social and political concerns. Colleges and universities can have an important and positive impact upon the lives of their students, but they need to recognize that this requires significant new efforts, as the number, diversity, attitudes, and life-styles of their students continue to change.

References

American College Testing Program. "Class Profile Service." In *ACT Research Services*. Iowa City: The American College Testing Program, 1974.

Bayer, A.E., and Boruch, R.F., *The Black Student in American Colleges*. Washington, D.C.: American Council on Higher Education, 1969.

62

Carnegie Commission on Higher Education. *Opportunities for Women in Higher Education*. New York: McGraw-Hill, 1973, p. iii.

_____. *New Students and New Places*. New York: McGraw-Hill, 1971.

Centra, John A. *Black Students at Predominately White Colleges: A Research Description*. Princeton, N.J.: Educational Testing Service, 1970.

Chickering, Arthur. *Commuting Versus Resident Students*. San Francisco: Jossey-Bass, 1974.

Clark, B.R., and Trow, M. "Determinants of College Student Subculture." In Newcomb, T.M., and Wilson, E.K. (eds.), *College Peer Groups*, Chicago: Aldine, 1966, p. 20.

Cross, K. Patricia. *The Junior College Student: A Research Description*. Princeton, N.J.: Educational Testing Service, 1968.

_____. *Beyond the Open Door*. San Francisco: Jossey-Bass, 1972.

_____. "The New Learners." *Change Magazine*. February 1973, p. 32.

Educational Testing Service. From *College and University Environment Scales, Second Edition*. Copyright © 1962, 1969 by C. Robert Pace. All rights reserved. Reproduced by permission of Educational Testing Service, the publisher.

_____. From *College Student Questionnaires*. Copyright © 1965 by Educational Testing Service. All rights reserved. Reproduced by permission.

_____. From *Institutional Functioning Inventory—A Prospectus*. Copyright © 1970, 1972 by Educational Testing Service. All rights reserved. Reproduced by permission.

_____. *Survey of College Achievement*. Princeton, N.J., 1972.

Heist, Paul, and Yonge, George. *Omnibus Personality Inventory. Form F, Manual*. © 1962, 1968 by The Psychological Corporation, New York.

Howard, Bruce. "The Search for a Whole Life: II—Turning toward the Professions." *Change Magazine*. October 1974, p. 19.

Kauffman, Joseph. *The Student in Higher Education*. New Haven, Conn.: The Hazen Foundation, 1968.

Keniston, Kenneth. "Youth: A 'New' Stage of Life." *The American Scholar*. Autumn 1970, pp. 631-654.

Kintzer, Frederick. *Middleman in Higher Education*. San Francisco: Jossey-Bass, 1973.

Peterson, Richard E. *On a Typology of College Students*. Princeton, N.J.: Educational Testing Service, 1965; p. 6.

Rudolph, Frederick. "Neglect of Students as a Historical Tradition." In *The College and the Student*. Washington, D.C.: American Council on Education, 1966, p. 53. Reprinted with permission.

Sandeen, Arthur, and Goodale, Thomas. "The Transfer Student: A Research Report." *N.A.S.P.A. Journal*, April 1971.

Ward, Robert A. In Murphry, Cullen. "Turning away from the Status Syndrome." *Change Magazine*. October 1974, p. 14. Reprinted with permission.

Yankelovich, Daniel, and Clark, Ruth. "College and Non-College Youth Values." *Change Magazine*. September 1974.

4

The Impact of Institutions

One of the great ironies of American higher education is that academic programs are planned, implemented, and continued for years without much attention being given to the actual outcomes of these programs. Many faculty and academic planners have assumed that knowledge transmitted in the classroom will not only remain with students for some time, but will also have some wondrous transfer effect on their lives. Institutions and their faculty study almost everything except the impact that they and their programs have upon their own students. Too much has been assumed for too long about the effects of teaching and of the learning environment in higher education without periodic and careful assessments being done. Too often courses have been required at the undergraduate level because it was assumed or argued that "such knowledge is necessary to any truly educated person," or that "the course will equip the student to make intelligent political decisions in future years."

Harold Hodgkinson, Director of the National Institute for Education, has recently presented evidence that indicates the very limited effects of a required course in natural science for undergraduates. A large number of students were tested in these courses each week during the semester to assess their rate of learning the material. The learning curve clearly indicated almost no activity on the part of the students until the mid-semester exam, when a "flurry of last-minute studying" took place. Then the curve rapidly declined until the semester's final exam, and a similar pattern took place. The "forgetting curve" as measured by objective tests during the weeks after the course was completed indicated that extremely little of the course material was retained. Since one of the purported objectives of the course was to assist students to make wise decisions as citizens regarding science policies in society, Hodgkinson (1975) humorously suggested that all elections, to be most effective, should be held during final examinations, as a few weeks later, the students will have forgotten most of what they "learned"! It is not being suggested here by any means that colleges should not require courses in natural science, or any other academic discipline. It is being argued, however, that institutions must be realistic about what they can actually accomplish through their academic programs for undergraduates, and that they should do periodic and careful assessments of the outcomes of their programs.

Institutions do have measurable impacts upon their students, and a considerable amount of research evidence has existed for some time regarding these matters. However, there is not a great deal of evidence to indicate that this research has influenced educational planners and faculty members in a significant way. Going to college does make a difference in the lives of undergraduates, but these differences may occur for varying reasons and as a result of widely diverse educational experiences. The same educational program at one institution is likely to have different impacts on individual students, and the changes that occur in students may be a result of a wide and complex array of circumstances that are either unknown or very difficult to measure accurately.

If an institution is concerned about its undergraduates accomplishing more than mere quantitative accumulation of knowledge, it will make substantial efforts to understand the impact it has upon the lives of its students—their attitudes and values, their activities as alumni, their own assessment of their experiences in college. An institution can learn a great deal about its own learning environment and what aspects of it might need improvement if the undergraduate experience is to prove most beneficial. A college can manipulate its environment in ways to make it more likely to have desired impacts, but it must do so in a way that reflects the total learning environment, not just isolated courses here and there in various departments. A college can learn about the impacts other institutions seem to have upon their students, and can share data and results with them in cooperative efforts to understand the unique qualities of certain colleges that actually exist. Such information can be of great assistance to faculty, planners, and admissions personnel, as decisions are made about what programs to implement, what campus facilities to build, and which students to recruit and admit.

In American society, significant changes continue to occur in young people from the ages of 18 to 21. Not all these changes occur as a result of going to college, of course, and many young persons who do not go to college also exhibit changes in attitudes and values that are not entirely dissimilar to their friends in college. The differences that do exist should be understood by individual colleges so that desired outcomes can be reached that are the actual result of programs developed by the institution. The relationship of academic programs for undergraduates to later adult accomplishments should also be pursued by institutions. Colleges may like to take credit for later achievements of their graduates, and may give inaccurate or misleading impressions to their students about the effect of their programs. While there may be actual positive relationships between college programs and accomplishments later in life, real assessments in this area should be done in order to assist faculty and others in making realistic education plans.

The impact of institutions on students is an area of concern that has attracted a considerable amount of attention in recent years, as educators continue to search for ways to improve the actual experiences of students in ways that may affect their lives. For a program of undergraduate educa- tion to be dynamic and useful, a carefully planned program of assessment of outcomes is necessary. Only in this manner can an institution gain an actual understanding of what is happening to its students as a result of their college experiences.

The purpose of this chapter is to review the major research that exists in the area of the impact of institutions, and to comment on the implications of this research for administrators, faculty, student affairs administrators, and planners.

Research on the Impact of Institutions

For over forty years there have been informal observations made and formal studies conducted in the area of college impact upon students. The results of these many studies of student change and stability, done at different universities, vary of course. Yet, as Feldman (1972) points out, certain consistencies in the findings can be found. Average freshman-to-senior changes in several characteristics have been occurring with considerable regularity in most American colleges and universities in recent decades. Thus, a large number of investigations all show that during their college years, students, on the average, decline in authoritarianism, dogmatism, and prejudice. Moreover, it has been clearly established that students typically become more liberal with regard to social, economic, and political issues. In addition, they come to value aesthetic experiences more highly. Freshman-to-senior changes such as these indicate an increasing openness to multiple aspects of the contemporary world, presumably paralleling wider ranges of knowledge, contact, and experiences associated with higher education. Declining commitment to religion, especially in its more orthodox forms, is also apparent. Certain trends of personality changes—particularly trends toward greater independence, self-confidence, and readiness to express impulses—are the rule rather than the exception. These trends are generally confirmed when students at a particular class level, say seniors, are asked if and how they have changed while at college.

Of course, a concern for the impacts that colleges have upon students includes a presumption about goals for higher education. Most faculty feel that colleges ought to have certain educational goals; thus, students should reflect these goals in some way upon graduation. Although colleges are very different from each other, most educators would probably agree that knowledge of subject matter, reading ability, effective use of the language, and the ability to solve problems and to think critically are important objectives for higher education (Lenning, Munday, and Maxey, 1969). However, Dressel and Mayhew (1954) feel that colleges need to go beyond the cognitive in their educational objectives, and argue that students should strive to develop a code of behavior based upon ethical principles. They further emphasize the need for increased international understanding, the human implications of science, and the appreciation of the fine arts.

Each institution, of course, needs to define its particular goals and purposes, so that its educational program can have the kinds of impacts upon its students that are intended. Quite often, institutions may find that, despite rather clear intentions and well-defined goals, they are not having the intended impact. More often, institutions do not have any reliable or realistic information concerning the impact of their programs, and they continue to teach and offer programs with the assumption that they are having the desired impact.

Despite the extensive research that has been done for many years on the impact of institutions, not all of it is reliable. There are different interpretations that can be made concerning some of it, and there are difficulties in measuring and interpreting change and stability during college years. As Withey (1971) points out, college attendance is but one of many influences on the lives of people and not necessarily the most significant. As Feldman and Newcomb (1969) argue, a common weakness of impact studies is that researchers have focused on differences between means, and that average change or the differences between mean scores of, say, freshmen and seniors, may obscure both the amount and the direction of individual change. An example is provided in a research study conducted by Miller (1959). Using the Allport-Vernon-Lindzey study of values, she found almost no difference between the scores of seniors and first-year students over a four-year period. However, individual changes on the scale ranged from −19 points to −16 points. These highly important changes, however, were canceled out in the reporting of average scores. Differences between mean scores do occur in many of these studies, and in significant and consistent directions; however, Feldman and Newcomb (1969), in summarizing the research in this area, express their preference for longitudinal studies as opposed to cross-sectional ones.

There are other problems as well. Viewing the consistent changes that have taken place among college students for many years regarding political and economic liberalism, Smith (1948) argues that some students become quite sophisticated about test taking, and they adjust their attitudes in accordance with professors' preferences. They may learn that liberalism is the expected response.

Withey (1971) points out that one should have reservations, too, about the accuracy of data obtained from reports by people with different educational backgrounds (for example, in studies comparing college and non-college youth). Many respondents with considerable educational experience are more proficient in completing surveys than the less well educated. The skills that are required to fill out most studies and questionnaires are the kinds of skills learned at the most advanced educational levels.

It is impossible, of course, to know and measure all the factors that may influence a student over a period of time. Quite often, the absence of change in a particular area may be significant, and even intended, but may be viewed by others as a "failure" of the college to effect a change. Some institutions may seek out and admit students who, at the time of entry, already have the kinds of characteristics, attitudes, and values that the college desires in its graduates. When the students graduate four years later, the "impact" of the college may have been very negligible, and might not have really enhanced their development or achievement (Astin, 1968b). However, some persons may claim that the attitudes and values of the graduates of such institutions are the result of their experiences there. As will be described later, the student inputs at time of entry are a very major influence upon the kinds of impacts that take place during college. The highly significant questions that Jacob (1957) has raised about changes that occur among college students' attitudes and values should be mentioned finally under this section on difficulties in measuring and interpreting change, although they will be reviewed in more detail later. What many colleges might have claimed as their special impact upon their students, Jacob viewed as the general impact of societal events. He argued that the attitudes college students expressed were merely a reflection of the expected and socially acceptable values of the current time.

Despite these problems in measurement and interpretation, there is a good deal of reliable and consistent reportable data that can be of considerable value in understanding the impact of institutions. The review of the major research will be reported in the following specific categories:

1. Changes in attitudes and values
2. The impact of different types of institutions
3. The influence of residence and peer groups
4. The impact of the faculty
5. A comparison of college students and noncollege attenders
6. The persistence of changes among students
7. The relationship between college achievement and adult accomplishment

Changes in Attitudes and Values

Nevitt Sanford (1967) has suggested that colleges encourage personal development by stimulating the imagination, fostering the development of the ego, and creating a greater awareness of human values. But, as he argues elsewhere (1962), personality development does not just happen automatically. The individual must be open for change, and the institution must provide the adequate stimulation in its educational program. This "readiness" is crucial to personality development in college. It is conceivable that the subsequent development of the entering college student rests more on her or his predisposition toward change than on any other factor.

As will be pointed out in this section, there is a good deal of evidence that indicates that colleges do have a significant impact on the attitudes and values of college students. In reviewing this evidence, it is useful to keep in mind Sanford's comments about the "state of readiness" among entering students. As it was presented in Chapter 3, the "new" students to higher education represent young people and others who have not traditionally been part of colleges and university life. It is quite likely that many of these "new" students exhibit different "states of readiness" than most traditional students have. Indeed, one of the most fruitful areas of research needed now on impact studies is the effect of institutional programs upon the attitudes and values of these new students.

Clearly the most prominent work in many years on the topic of changes in attitudes and values during the college years was Jacob's (1957) survey of investigations. He argued that there was a profile of values which held true for 75 to 80 percent of all American college students. He said that the students were "gloriously contented" in their present activity and in their outlook toward the future. Students were described as "unabashedly self-centered," aspiring above all to material gratifications for themselves and their families. Though conventionally middle-class, they had an "easy tolerance of diversity," and they were ready to live in a society without racial, ethnic, or income barriers. The traditional moral virtues, such as sincerity, honesty, and loyalty, were highly valued, but there was little inclination to censor laxity, which students considered to be widespread. A need for religion was generally recognized, but students did not expect religious beliefs to govern their daily decisions. Rather they expected that these decisions would be socially determined. The general tendency was to be "dutifully responsive toward government," but there was little inclination to contribute voluntarily to the public welfare or to seek an influential role in public affairs. According to Jacob, students set great stock in college in general and in their own college in particular, with vocational preparation and skills and experience in social relations being regarded as the greatest benefits of college education. Finally, Jacob argued that there were few actual significant changes in values during the college years, and that among the few changes that could be noted the most striking were in the direction of greater conformity with the prevailing profile.

Jacob's study attracted a considerable amount of attention from the public and from leaders in higher education. Although his work has been criticized from a number of points of view (e.g., Riesman, 1958), it stimulated a great deal of discussion about the purposes of colleges and universities, especially as these purposes related to students' attitudes and values. Since Jacob's study, a large number of investigations have been done. Regarding the reported "changes" in students' attitudes and values, and the "increased liberalization" of their thinking, Jacob remained skeptical. He interpreted the changes in college as reflecting an adaptation to a college norm that mirrored the larger societal norm, rather than the development of an internalized commitment in this area. He argued that students changed in accordance with the dominant social pressure of the times. They learned quite naturally while in college that it was inappropriate to display certain attitudes, such as prejudice. He claimed that to call this process a liberalization of student values is a misnomer. The impact of the college experience is rather to socialize the individual, to refine, polish, and "shape up" his/her values so that he or she can fit comfortably into the ranks of American college alumni. At least one researcher since that time (Korn, 1968) has arrived at a conclusion very similar to Jacob's. Studying freshman-to-senior changes, he concluded that changes in attitudes and values seemed more a process of socialization than of personality restructuring. Jacob argued that "value changes" simply reflect a time when the culture as a whole is changing in these directions. After experiencing the tumultous decade of the 1960s and observing the events on college campuses during that time, a rather convincing case can be made for the notion that "society sets the agenda" for college students. The attitudes expressed by large numbers of college students during this time regarding the government and its policies were very different from those expressed when Jacob conducted his investigations during the 1950s. Were these differences in attitudes a function of personality changes that took place as a result of the college curriculum and educational program, or did they simply reflect existing problems in society? There is, perhaps, no final answer to such questions. Despite the fact that Jacob expressed skepticism about how attitudes and values change in college, the evidence is, nevertheless, that change does occur, even though the change might not be the result of carefully considered, internalized thinking and feeling on the part of students.

One of the most frequently used instruments in the measurement of attitude and value change has been the Allport-Vernon-Lindzey study of values (1960, 1970). This research instrument was designed to measure six basic interests or motives in personality. These basic interests are theoretical, economic, aesthetic, social, political, and religious. The instrument attempts to assess the relative strength of each of these six values within a person.

Huntley (1965) used this instrument in an extensive investigation of 1,027 undergraduate men. He found that seniors had changed since their first year, and that differences among curricular groups at time of entry continued and were sharpened during the college years. He attempted to pay close attention to individual patterns of change so that such differences might not cancel each other out in total populations. Thus, he grouped the subjects by their academic fields of concentration at time of graduation: English, economics, government, premedicine, physics, and engineering.

The English majors, as did the other five groups, revealed a highly significant gain on the aesthetic value during the four years of college, and it should be noted that their gain was greater than that of any other group. They stood higher than all other groups on the aesthetic value at entrance, and this gap widened over the four years. Similarly, they ranked lowest of the six groups on the economic value, and this trend also tended to be accentuated by the time of graduation. English majors, like all other five groups, showed a marked and statistically significant decrease on the religious value.

As might be expected, the economics majors ranked the economic value the highest. At entrance, they outranked all others and showed a significant gain over the four years. They were low on the theoretical value, and at graduation they were next to the lowest on the aesthetic value, outranking only the engineers.

The government majors lead all others on the political value, both at entrance and at graduation. They ranked the lowest of the groups on the theoretical value. They ranked highest on the social value at time of graduation, although the difference between their score and that of others was not striking.

The premedical students exhibited a high score on the theoretical value at entrance, and compared with other groups, this trend became accentuated over the four years. They showed a significant decrease on the economic value and a decided gain on the aesthetic.

The physics majors clearly outranked all the others on the theoretical value, both at entrance and at graduation. This high standing on the theoretical value is balanced by their standing lowest on the political value at entrance and moving still lower at graduation.

The students majoring in engineering, while ranking second to the economics majors on the economic value at entrance and at graduation, stood lowest on the aesthetic value, and gained the least in this area during the four years.

In terms of a summary of changes in value scores, each group decreased significantly on the religious value and increased on the aesthetic value. But it is still difficult to know if these changes were the actual result of academic course work, social-personal influences, or simply maturation.

In another valuable study conducted at Michigan State University (Lehmann, 1963), seniors were asked how they were different from the way they were as first-year students, and most said they considered themselves more tolerant of others different from themselves, and a majority also felt that they were more interested in intellectual and cultural matters. Only abut 1 student in 5 expressed a stronger commitment to religion, but most claimed they felt much more responsible for their own behavior.

Nevitt Sanford's classic impact studies (1956) of Vassar College students emphasized changes in personality closely associated with attitudes and values. Students showed large decreases in ethnocentrism and authoritarianism over the four years. Many of the first-year students scored relatively high on the authoritarian scale, one that has been described as anti-intellectual by Sanford. The fact that many of these high scorers were changeable is encouraging for educators. There were significant changes noted in three other scales in the Vassar study that merit a brief description. Low scorers on the Social Maturity scale are compulsive, rigid, punitive, and conventional. High scorers are relatively free of these characteristics. On the Impulse Expression scale, high scorers have a greater readiness to express impulses, or to seek gratification of them in overt action or in conscious feeling and attitude. Finally, the Developmental Status scale indicates that high scorers are flexible and uncompulsive, critical of the institutional authority of family, state, and religion, and mature in their interests. On all three scales, students exhibited significant gains in scores during college. Similar findings have been reported at different types of colleges on these scales (Webster, Freedman, and Heist, 1962).

In a very extensive study done by Bayer, Royer, and Webb (1973) as part of the American Council on Education's Cooperative Institutional Research Program, over 60,000 students were sampled in an effort to assess how they were affected by the colleges they attended. A large amount of data has been collected in the ACE program, and through 1972, some 2 million first-year college students had participated in the research study. Follow-up surveys are conducted on these freshmen that cover student experiences and achievements, aspirations and plans for the future, perceptions and evaluations of the college environment, and educational outcomes and academic standing. The findings of this study with regard to college impact indicate that on most social and campus issues, more liberal attitudes prevail than at the time of entry to college. In terms of some specific issues, it is noteworthy that in 1967, over one-half agreed that the activities of married women are best confined to the home and family; in 1971, less than one-fourth endorsed this position. On the issue of population growth, about two-fifths of the students agreed that parents should be discouraged from having large families; four years later, more than three-fourths agreed. Again, the question is raised about these changes being the result of the college experience, or merely a reflection of the dominant social trends of the times. As will be described later, Feldman and Newcomb (1969) show that some of these same changes also take place among individuals who have not attended college, although typically to a lesser degree.

Arthur Chickering (1968), as director of the project on student development in small colleges, conducted an intensive study of students in thirteen colleges. He found that seniors were generally rated higher than first-year students on the following dimensions: goal directedness, personal stability and integration, openness to experience, resourcefulness, and persistence. Chickering's study has special significance, because it included a variety of assessment techniques, including personal interviews over a period of time.

No Time for Youth is a publication by Katz and associates (1969) that has attracted a good deal of attention. It is based on an intensive study of college students over a four-year period. Data were obtained from several thousand students, and a random group of over 200 students was selected for intensive interviews by a staff of experienced psychologists. The students were interviewed at least two times each year about their academic and nonacademic experiences and the meaning these had for them. The study includes a vast amount of useful and readable information about students. The study revealed that students demonstrate more independence, self-understanding, liberalism, and tolerance as seniors than they did as freshmen. The case materials in the book provide a valuable insight into the nature of the college experience for individual students.

It is clear that the college experience does have an impact upon the attitudes and values of students. Withey (1971) has effectively summarized the research in this area:

the college experience appears more likely than not to make students more open-minded and liberal, less concerned with material possessions, more concerned with aesthetic and cultural values, more relativistic and less moralistic, but more integrated, rational, and consistent.

The Impact of Different Types of Institutions

As Gurin (1971) has pointed out, too few of the studies involving college students and how they change have been done in terms of comparisons among different types of institutions. Most have been done, in fact, at single institutions. A weakness in some of the cross-institutional studies that have been conducted is that the factor of selection has not been accounted for adequately. Gurin does argue, however, that values of students seem to change regardless of the nature of the college, and that there are differential effects that are consistent with the dominant academic and social atmosphere of the college.

Emphasis in these studies in recent years has focused on the college environment or climate, more than on traditional characteristics; that students have widely varying perceptions of college environments has been well documented (e.g., Pace and Stern, 1958) for some time. After studying a large number of students at hundreds of colleges, Astin (1968a) reported that there are different "images" that students have of various college environments. The universities had highly competitive peer environments, a low participation in musical and artistic activities, a lack of cohesion among the students, and rather lax student conduct regulations. The dominant feature of the university classroom is that there is little personal contact between the students and the professors. Most students at these large universities perceived that there was little personal concern for them as individuals.

The liberal arts colleges had images quite different from the universities. They were viewed as being strong on cohesiveness and personal cooperation because of close relationships between students and faculty. Most significantly, the students perceived high degree of personal concern for them on the part of the college.

Students in the teacher's colleges enjoyed a good deal of leisure time, and experienced rather stringent disciplinary rules. Most importantly, the students perceived a low level of academic competitiveness.

The peer environment in the technological institutions reflects a high degree of independence and competitiveness. Flexibility in the academic program is viewed as minimal by the students, and social activities are given comparatively little emphasis.

Although there are obviously important differences among these types of institutions, there is a need for extensive longitudinal research to assess the differential impacts of these environments. Astin and Panos (1969) have conducted the major work in this area, studying a large sample of students in order to determine how a student's persistence in college, career plans, achievements, and educational aspirations are affected by the type of college she or he attends. Regarding universities, they concluded that students there are more likely to drop out and to lower their educational aspirations. They argue that this is due to a considerable degree to the lack of personal relationships between students and faculty, and to the rather low level of personal concern perceived by the undergraduates.

The students in the liberal arts colleges tended to remain in the institution, and their educational aspirations increase while they were enrolled. This was attributed, at least in part, to the more personal nature of the campus environment.

Students attending the technological institutions were strongly influenced to pursue engineering or related fields and were steered away from careers in medicine, business, and law. Their educational aspirations remained more stable during college than students in the universities and in the liberal arts colleges.

One of the most interesting, yet relatively unexpected, results of the study was that the seniors' scores on the Graduate Record Examination were not influenced by the intellectual level of the students enrolled at the institution, or by the perceived level of academic competitiveness there. Finally, it was found that differences in academic achievement as measured by tests given during the senior year were much more a result of academic differences that existed when these students entered the institution rather than being due to some special aspect of the college's overall program.

Trent and Medsker (1968) compared students in different types of institutions: public, private nonsectarian, and private religious colleges and universities. In all types of institutions, they found that the students shifted in their scores on social maturity (their measure of the nonauthoritarian syndrome) between their first and senior years. In a study of students at Antioch, Reed, Swarthmore, San Francisco State, Berkelely, University of the Pacific, St. Olaf, and the University of Portland, McConnell (1962) found that seniors were higher in civil libertarianism than first-year students. The results indicate that students seem to change to about the same degree regardless of the college they attended.

Arthur Chickering (1970) has noted the interesting paradox that, because of selection factors, sometimes absolute change on some measures of attitudes and values is actually greater in those institutions stressing these values *less* than in those institutions where these values form a dominant part of the institutional climate. The latter colleges attract students who already score so high on that value that they have much less "room to move" than the students attending the former colleges. This seems to lend to a conclusion that the "best colleges have the least effect."

Feldman and Newcomb (1969) propose accentuation as a general principle applying to the impact of the different subenvironments within an institution:

Whatever the characteristics of any individual that selectively propel him toward particular educational settings—going to college, selecting a particular one, choosing a certain academic major, acquiring membership in a particular group of peers—those same characteristics are apt to be reinforced and extended by the experiences incurred in those selected settings.

In a study referred to earlier, Chickering (1970) followed the same students for four years at twelve small colleges that differed greatly in their goals, climate, rules, teaching, and value orientations of their faculty. Despite this diversity, Chickering noted a great deal of commonality in the changes students underwent. Such changes as increased autonomy, increased aesthetic sensitivity and interest, increased tolerance for ambiguity and complexity, and increased religious liberalism were found in virtually all the colleges. These changes occurred at highly organized institutions with numerous regulations and close adult supervision. They also occurred at a "student-centered" college with little overt structure, few regulations, and minimum adult supervision. At two traditional colleges—one poor and relatively unknown operating with limited facilities, the other wealthy, prestigious with ample facilities and resources—similar changes occurred. Similar changes also occurred at two nontraditional colleges, one emphasizing independent studies and flexible programming devleoped by students themselves, the other with a highly structured curriculum using many required courses and a complex system of comprehensive examinations.

Very few studies have been conducted on the impact of community colleges on students. The available evidence suggests that students in community colleges undergo the same kinds of changes, but to a lesser extent, as students in four-year institutions. This seems to hold even when community college students are compared with students after an experience of two years in the four-year college. For example, Plant (1962) showed that students in the four-year colleges changed more after two years on scales such as dogmatism than junior college students after a comparable period. There have been great growth and considerable change among community colleges in the past ten years, and additional study is needed to assess the impacts that these institutions have.

Feldman and Newcomb (1969) have found that the conditions for campuswide impacts occur most often in small, residential, four-year colleges. Relative homogeneity of students and faculty and frequent interaction between these two groups are important conditions for impact. State universities usually attract students that are very heterogeneous, and the faculty is often so large and diverse that uniform effects regarding impact are infrequent. However, various smaller segments of large universities may have significant influences upon students. Unfortunately, most of these impacts have occurred more by chance than by design, or by conscious planning by the institution.

In summary, students do change in rather consistent directions in their attitudes and values during four years of college, regardless of the college they attended. Certain distinctive colleges, noted mainly for their small size, homogeneity, and careful student selection, may have more marked impacts upon their students in certain areas, such as encouraging graduate study. Student impact factors appear to be more significant in later outcomes than does the college experience itself. The role of the college serves, in many cases, to accentuate the attitudes, values, and achievements that students who select that particular institution anticipate.

The Influence of Residence and Peer Groups

There has been an interest for a long time in the influence of the "student culture" on academic life and educational outcomes. Although few educators doubt the significant role that student culture plays, there are many problems in assessing accurately the real influences of peer groups among undergraduate students. Peer group influence may actually work at cross purposes with the academic program of the college, or it may be an effective vehicle for it. Many of the studies in this area have focused on comparisons between various types of residences at one point in time. Moreover, differences among students living in various kinds of residences often are the result of the student selection and recruitment process more than any other factors.

Despite these difficulties, there is still a good deal of interest among researchers in this area. It is evident that a considerable share of what happens to change students during the college years is a function of student-to-student contact. The research in this area over the years has encouraged many educators to think beyond the classroom walls to the "campus environment" as a learning system.

Theodore Newcomb has been the pioneer researcher in the area of student peer group influence in higher education. His studies of how personality changes take place within a student community (Newcomb, 1943), and several other studies (e.g., Newcomb and Wilson, 1966) since then are classics in the field. Newcomb has concluded that what students learn in college is determined in large measure by their fellow students or, more precisely, by the norms of behavior, attitudes, and values that prevail in their living groups. He also suggests that the college peer group helps to shape the general behavior of individuals and is also a strong influence on classroom attainment as well. The relationships among students are significant factors in their general attitude toward the college.

Newcomb argues that size, homogeneity, isolation, and shared attitudes are major factors that affect the influences groups have upon individuals. Colleges that desire to have an impact upon student attitudes by working partially through the peer environment should attempt to encourage small groups, and ones that are fairly similar in social class, sex, or religious affiliation. If these small groups are in some way isolated from other groups that do not share their attitudes, their own convictions might be reinforced further. The student selection process, both formal and informal, on many campuses enhances this situation. Often, the college may not like the kinds of influence it observes upon students within the peer environment, as the impact may be primarily conservative or provincial in nature. However, the college can exert an important influence by careful planning and student selection. Almost in spite of any conscious efforts on the part of college officials, student peer group influence occurs. Instead of ignoring this process, the college can benefit by seeking to understand it, and to work to make it consistent with its purposes.

Astin (1968), in his studies of the college environment, has concluded that from the point of view of the college student, the stimuli provided by her/his peers may be the most important part of the college experience. Of course, students spend more time with each other than with any other group of people on the campus, so it is perhaps not surprising to learn that their influence upon each other is considerable. Astin also suggests that students who reside with other students on the campus are likely to be influenced more in their attitudes and values while in college than those students who live at home. Astin's work involved several thousand students at 246 institutions.

In a sequel study, Astin and Panos (1969) found that peers have a significant influence upon educational and vocational plans. As students progressed through college, their academic concentrations tended to conform more and more to those in their friendship group. If a high percentage of one's friends choose a particular career, the probability is quite good that a student might be influenced to do the same. They also found that the cohesiveness of the peer environment (measured primarily in terms of the number of fellow students whom the student regards as close friends) has a pronounced positive effect on persistence in college. By contrast, colleges with relatively incohesive peer environments have dropout rates that are much higher than predicted from their student inputs. Attending a college with a cohesive environment also appears to increase the student's interest in pursuing a career in science.

The longitudinal study of Vassar College by Sanford (1962) has made important contributions to the knowledge about the effect of student peer groups. Sanford's data indicated that the role of student peer groups is of fundamental significance in determining the course of events in the college experience. Bushnell (1962), who was also associated with the Vassar study, has emphasized the existence of two cultures on the campus: the student culture and the faculty culture. Insofar as these two cultures are in competition or conflict in their efforts to socialize the new student, Bushnell tends to see the student culture as the "victor." It has a major influence on the college experience.

Marjorie Lozoff (1969), working as part of the research team on the influential "Stanford Student Study" (Katz and Associates, 1969), has written an excellent article on residential groups and individual development of students. She argues that the residential milieu has a strong effect on the undergraduate student. It may either aid or retard his/her social, academic, and emotional development. She suggests further that the educational goals of a campus cannot be achieved during the few hours a week that the student is in the classroom, and that the extracurricular experiences of the student are relevant to both his/her developmental and educational goals. The research team in this study conducted intensive interviews with the same students over a period of four years, and was impressed with the extent to which the relationship between the social environment of the students and intellectual receptivity was noted by them. Most of the students indicated that a great deal of their mental and psychic energy was involved in developing a sense of their own uniqueness. The residence groups to which they belonged played an important part in defining the patterns of adaptation.

Dressel and Lehmann (1965), in a study at Michigan State University, found that the most significant reported experience in the collegiate lives of the students was their association with different personalities in their living unit. The analysis of interview and questionnaire data suggested that discussions and bull sessions were a potent factor in shaping the attitudes and values of these students.

Douglas Heath (1968) studied student development at Haverford College over a four-year period, using a variety of research techniques, including the participant observer method. He concluded that change in students during college is mediated primarily by the quality of one's personal relationships with others and the expectations that others have of the type of person one should become. He argued that the college program is liberating for the students to the extent there is a communal character to it and an internal coherency of purpose.

Astin (1973) did an interesting study of the impact of dormitory living on students, and found that living in a dormitory, compared with living at home, had positive benefits on the student's education. Dormitory residents were less likely to drop out than commuters, more likely to apply for admission to graduate school and to earn a high grade point average. Living in a dormitory also increased the chances that students would be satisfied with their overall undergraduate experience, particularly in the area of interpersonal contacts with faculty and other students.

Chickering (1974) has written a valuable book on the differences between commuter and resident students. In his extensive study, he found that there are significant differences between the two groups regarding attitudes toward the college and perceptions of the educational experience. Resident students are influenced considerably more by the institution than are commuting students, and they also have much more contact with faculty members and out-of-class cocurricular programs. The results of his study suggest that if a college wants to maximize its impact on all its students, it might consider some short-term on-campus living experiences for its commuter students.

Chickering (1969) has also written a very influential book, *Education and Identity*, in which he describes seven major vectors of student development and considers these vectors in relation to six major aspects of the college environment. The seven vectors of development are: (1) developing competence, (2) managing emotions, (3) developing autonomy, (4) establishing identity, (5) freeing interpersonal relationships, (6) developing purpose, and (7) developing integrity. The six conditions for impact are: (1) clarity and consistency of objectives; (2) institutional size; (3) curriculum, teaching, and evaluation; (4) residence hall arrangements; (5) faculty and administration; and (6) friends, groups, and student culture. His thesis is not that all students change along with equal force for all students at all institutions, but that such changes do occur for some students and they can occur more frequently for others. Environmental conditions at some institutions do foster or inhibit such changes, and systematic modification can increase the frequency of value development. Chickering summarizes the influence of friends, groups, and the student culture by indicating that they play a major role in shaping the attitudes of students toward the college and in affecting their own development.

In summary, it is clear that the impact of the student culture can be considerable on the educational attitudes and behavior of undergraduates. Although there is considerable evidence that students are influenced by the interpersonal environment that exists at the college, it is less clear to what extent these findings reflect different environmental impact rather than selection. As Gurin (1971) notes, much of the peer-socialization research has consisted of intensive studies within a single institution. He argues that what is now needed is research on student peer influence with multi-institutional designs. In this manner, a better perspective might be gained on the role that social influence processes play in the value changes that students undergo.

Student peer influence can be sufficiently influential on a campus that it has a major impact on the educational program. A sensitive faculty and administration will take careful note of this influence and attempt to arrange the educational environment in ways that can enhance student growth.

The Impact of the Faculty

Perhaps one of the most difficult—and important—aspects to measure of the college's impact upon students is the influence of faculty. Teaching, of course, is the basic function of the undergraduate institution, and it has been assumed for as long as there have been colleges that the major intellectual influence upon students is exerted by the faculty. A professor's impact upon a student may be in the form of increased understanding or knowledge, motivation or self-confidence, or personal insight and curiosity. Faculty influence may not really occur until the student is out of college, or it might be the result of an intense, personal learning activity, such as a weekend retreat or seminar. Lectures and research projects are likely to have a significant influence upon some students, while others respond more to personal encouragement on a day-to-day basis from faculty they admire. Much of the impact the faculty members may have upon students may not be consciously realized by students themselves. Decisions about future professional plans or about one's political, social, and religious values may be considerably influenced by questions raised by faculty members. Such "impact," of course, is very difficult to measure, as many students report in studies that they have "worked these matters out for themselves." The manner in which such decisions are made, the alternatives that are considered, and the consequences that are forseen may be greatly influenced by faculty members. Despite these difficulties in "quantifying" the impact of faculty, there are some valuable studies that can be reported. As Astin (1968) noted, although the undergraduate student generally spends less time attending class than she or he does engaging in other campus activities, the stimuli provided by the classroom experience are probably among the most significant sources of influence during the undergraduate years. The difficult-to-define, but immensely important potential influence of the faculty member upon a student is illustrated by this brief account of a student at Hofstra (Raushenbush, 1964) in an interview:

Professor Anderson did everything for me. He taught me how to think . . . how to take one step at a time to find out what you want to know—the wonderful experience of being able to do that. He didn't answer questions; he said, "what are the alternatives?" But he helped you along . . . he got you to work on every possibility, one after another.

This professor did not have to be a close personal friend of the student's or his personal psychological counselor to be effective. The teacher was influential because his competence, his concern, and his own dedication to his subject matter were obvious to his students. His willingness to share his experience was complete.

Unfortunately, as is well known, such growth-producing relationships do not exist very often for large numbers of undergraduates at many institutions. Too often, the educational experience is impersonal and lonely, and students do not come into frequent or meaningful contact with faculty. Chickering (1969) mentions four general conditions conducive to productive relationships among students and faculty—accessibility, authenticity, knowledge, and the ability to talk with a student—and that these conditions are not complicated to arrange. He goes on to point out, however, that at many universities such arrangements will require modifications of current practices. Large numbers of students at large public universities report that they have very little contact with faculty in situations where faculty express an interest in their educational problems (Underwood, 1968).

Burton Clark (1965) views the effectiveness of the college experience as the extent to which faculty values have gained control over the values of the extracurriculum. Although he is not negative to the contributions that the student culture can make to the educational program, he quotes Woodrow Wilson (1925) to make his point about the role of the faculty: "The comradeship of undergraduates will never breed the spirit of learning. The circle must be widened. It must include . . . the teachers." It may be just as important to bring the extracurriculum under the control of the college as it is to revise academic courses if the institution is to influence its students in planned ways. Colleges where the faculty has the greatest influence upon these matters are those where the maximum intellectual impact takes place.

Perhaps it is inevitable that there are differences between student and faculty values. Wallace (1966) argues that since faculty and students represent different age groups and generations, the interaction between the two is really a "bureaucratized confrontation of generations." Feldman and Newcomb (1969) summarized a number of studies that show, rather consistently, the manner in which faculty and students do differ. Students place more value than faculty on such goals and activities as vocational training, developing social competence and social graces, participating in extracurricular activities, and developing a personal philosophy. Faculty, on the other hand, place more emphasis than students on such goals for students as developing intellectual and moral capacities, achieving academically, acquiring skills and knowledge necessary to participate as an effective citizen, understanding world issues and pressing social, political, and economic problems.

Although large numbers of students have commented upon the depersonalized teaching environments in various institutions, it is not necessarily true that these same students desire it to be otherwise. There is some evidence (Spaights, 1967) to indicate that students who achieve at the highest levels academically desire much more personal contact with faculty than do low achievers. Students, for the most part, do not desire close, personal friendship from faculty; and faculty socialize most often with their peers. What students do desire and need, however, is an effective learning relationship with faculty, so that they can mature intellectually under the guidance of an expert who knows them and cares about their growth.

As Feldman and Newcomb (1969) point out, there is a good deal of evidence to indicate that faculty are particularly important in influencing occupational decisions and educational aspirations. Faculty usually rank along with parents as being the most important influences in such decisions. Faculty appear to be of greater importance in certain career areas than in others. They are particularly influential in the decisions of students to become college teachers. Grigg (1965) found that students who reported frequent talks with a faculty member were much more likely to be planning on going to graduate or professional school than were students who reported infrequent talks. Gurin and Katz (1966), in a study of ten colleges, found that end-of-year first-year students who reported most contact with teachers had significantly higher occupational aspirations than other students. Students in different curricula appear to have varying views of what they consider effective teaching. In a study at Brooklyn College (Riley, Ryan, and Lifshitz, 1950), for example, it was found that for students in the arts, the three most important qualities were knowledge of the subject, ability to encourage thought, and enthusiasm. For the physical and biological sciences, they were ability to explain, organization, and knowledge of the subject. For the social sciences, they were ability to encourage thought, organization, and tolerance toward student disagreement.

Students usually feel that faculty members have more influence than their fellow students on their educational and career development. However, they most often feel that their fellow students are more important in their personality development than faculty.

Chickering (1969) has summarized his studies of student and faculty influence by asserting that the most important ingredient of impact is the faculty itself:

When individual faculty members talk with students—when they are accessible, authentic, and reasonably knowledgeable about students—friendships, reference groups, and the student culture receive continued stimulation, support, and challenge. For the behavior, views, and values of these adults, when visible, are much discussed. It is the faculty who ultimately determine the force and substance of student culture. Whatever the college is, and whatever it becomes—whether it lives, dies, or suffers dramatic mutation—follows primarily from their decisions and behavior.

Although the impact of the faculty upon students may be extremely difficult to measure, additional attention and research is needed in this area, for there is no more important aspect of the educational process than the role of the faculty.

A Comparison of College Students and Non-College Attenders

As has been mentioned earlier, the fact that changes do take place in students during college does not necessarily mean that the college experience is exclusively responsible for the change. One of the most frequent designs used to overcome this measurement problem is to compare college attenders with non-college attenders. Of course, the two "groups" are not completely comparable and cannot be equated on all relevant factors that influence the decision to go to college. As Gurin (1971) has noted, such a comparative study at least takes into consideration such obvious factors as socioeconomic background, academic ability, and initial position on the attitude and value scale by which change is being measured. Although there have not been a large number of well-done studies in this area, a few of the most important findings will be reported.

Clark Kerr (1971), in the preface to one of the Carnegie Commission reports, summarizes much of the research in this area by concluding that individuals who go to college tend to be more liberal and tolerant in their attitudes, more satisfied with their jobs, more highly paid and less subject to unemployment, more thoughtful and deliberate in their consumer expenditures, more likely to vote and to participate in community activities, and more informed about community, national, and world affairs. Of course, these are fairly general statements, many of them simply outcomes of the fact that college graduates have access to certain jobs that non-college graduates do not.

Plant (1965), in studies comparing students who attended San Jose State University with others who applied, but did not attend college, found that both groups made statistically significant decreases in authoritarianism, dogmatism, and ethnocentrism. In further analyzing the data, he discovered that these were differences between the two groups at entrance, however, and that the college attenders changed more dramatically than the non-college attenders on the three scales. From this, Plant argues that—at least on some characteristics—the college experience had a "facilitative effect" upon changes rather than a unique one.

Clearly the most extensive and important study comparing college students with nonattenders was done by Trent and Medsker (1968). They sampled over 10,000 high school seniors in 37 high schools in 16 communities in California, Pennsylvania, Illinois, Indiana, and other states. They then tested a large percentage of this same group four years later, and compared those who had attended college with those who had not gone to college and who had spent most of their time working.

Trent and Medsker found that the nonattenders were more authoritarian than those who went to college after their senior year in high school. After four years, the nonattenders typically did not change in these attitudes, while the college attenders became significantly less authoritarian. Thus, the gap that existed in high school widened after four years. On a scale that measured intellectual disposition, the college attenders again scored higher than the non-college attenders while in high school. After four years, the college attenders tended to increase even further on this scale, while the nonattenders tended to *decline* from their previous position. Also, four years after high school graduation, a larger percentage of those in college reported a change in religious values than did those who were employed during this time. Of further interest, the high school women who did not attend college and who became homemakers upon graduation declined in intellectual disposition and nonauthoritarianism the most dramatically of any group. Trent and Medsker suggest that this finding gives some validity to the concept of the "trapped housewife."

These changes noted by Trent and Medsker generally remained even when differences in intellectual ability and socioeconomic status of the two groups were held constant. Students who attended college for a while and later dropped out also changed more in their attitudes and values than persons who did not attend college at all.

The findings from the Trent and Medsker study are very valuable, but there still remain some perplexing questions. Young persons who decide to go to college may reflect an openness that predisposes them to change, so that they would have changed even if they had not gone to college. Their study was done during the years 1959 to 1963, and, of course, there have been dramatic social and economic changes since that time. Attitudes toward work, new kinds of colleges, and the women's liberation movement are only three examples of changes that might have an influence on a similar study now. The changes described by Trent and Medsker may be viewed as encouraging and "in the right direction" by some educators, but as not sufficiently dramatic or consistent by others. It is, however, safe to conclude that there is some evidence now that many of the changes observed amoung college students are not just the reflection of a general maturational or cultural process common to all young people.

The Persistence of Change among Students

Perhaps the most meaningful evaluation of the value of going to college is an assessment of the activities and attitudes of graduates several years after college. Virtually everyone associated with higher education is interested in what happens to students in their postcollege years. For many people in the United States, the real value of going to college is measured by what happens to them and how they live after graudation. Despite these obvious observations, there have been very few studies of persistence of college impacts after college. Knowledge of such patterns would, of course, be of great value in understanding what colleges do to and for students in formulating educational goals and procedures.

Freedman (1967) has conducted one of the most valuable studies in this area. Concentrating on Vassar College students, he conducted an investigation of the attitudes and values of six different decades of alumnae. While he found variations in values and attitudes of the various classes, he tended to view the differences as a recolection of the changing values in American society over the period of two generations. For example, he noted an increase in authoritarianism in the class of 1956, and suggested that this was a reflection of the conservatism and American ethnocentrism of that period. He stated that while there was not conclusive evidence that these differences represent persistence of different attitudes and values acquired in college, they may be interesting indications of the values and attitudes current at the time the women were in college.

Feldman and Newcomb (1969) have concluded that on the basis of several studies, college-experienced changes in political, social, and economic attitudes, typically in the liberal direction, have been shown to persist, or even to be extended, after the college years. They also note that no studies have indicated significant reversals of such attitudes. Some other studies, most notably those of Freedman and Bereiter (1963), indicate that there may be postcollege reversals in such areas as religious attitudes and acceptance of the unconventional. After some of these students had been out of college a few years, they tended to become more traditional and conservative in their religious values. To some extent, they reflected their views before college attendance. It is, no doubt, reasonable to assume that these changes are the result of postcollege socialization with adults with similar views.

Perhaps the most significant study of persistence of change among students after college was done by Newcomb et al. (1967). In the 1960s, he interviewed the same women he had sampled in his classic Bennington College study (Newcomb, 1943) to see what had happened to their attitudes and values a generation later. He found a good deal of persistence in the attitudes of Bennington women, in particular, those who became less conservative in college tended to remain so a generation later. It was significant to note that persistence of a particular impact was closely related to involvement in a postcollege environment that was consistent with the earlier situation. The husbands of these women graduates were also important in terms of their attitudes, as they were very supportive of the same values that their wives had earlier. The likelihood that a particular value might persist was thus enhanced for a woman who married a man with similar attitudes. The Bennington women were able to maintain their college changes over the years, therefore, by choosing a social environment that was supportive of their expressed values.

For many people, college attendance is the most intensive period of interpersonal interaction and involvement with ideas and social issues. Moreover, the experience most often takes place as people are maturing into adulthood. The peer environment in college perhaps brings students into more intimate contact with large numbers of other people of varying backgrounds and views than at any other time of their lives. This is not to suggest that change does not or cannot take place after college. Most attitudes do not change casually, but in response to new experiences and information. As people mature and have more experiences, the less the relative impact of any specific incident usually is.

It is evident from these research studies that many of the attitudes and values acquired in college do persist for many years after graduation. It is also evident that this persistence may be a consequence of seeking out and living in postcollege environments that support these attitudes.

The Relationship between College Achievement and Adult Accomplishment

A concern with the impact of colleges and universities upon students logically extends to what the students actually accomplish in their lives after graduation. There have not been a large number of studies done in this area, and, of course, there are many problems associated with this kind of research. Opinions may vary widely as to the appropriate definition of "accomplishment" after college, and even if agreement is reached, it may be very difficult to assign some activity or experience in college as the stimulus or cause for the accomplishment. Nevertheless, there are some useful findings that need to be reported, because they may provide helpful insights and new perspectives on educational planning.

The research of Donald Hoyt (1965, 1966) is of central importance in this area. He concluded that college grades do not appear to be related to significant adult accomplishment, as measured by success in occupations such as engineering, teaching, business, and medicine. For example, the grades of medical school students appear unrelated to later success as physicians. Arguing that success in school work is not related to success outside of school, Hoyt suggests that to continue to promote academic accomplishment as the only form of educational success is to doom a large proportion of good students to mediocrity or failure. He reports that there are a number of talents and potentials which are valued by society and which are relatively independent of academic potential. Richards, Holland, and Lutz (1966) confirmed this conclusion in the measurement of various kinds of adult accomplishment, such as leadership, social service, and scientific achievement.

Another study needing mention was completed by Munday and Davis (1974) for the American College Testing Program. Although their research focused upon students in only three universities and evaluated adult accomplishments only a few years after college graduation, they also found these accomplishments to be uncorrelated with academic talent, including test scores and college grades. They suggest that this kind of information should lend educational institutions to acknowledge that there are many kinds of talents related to later success which might be identified and nurtured. They conclude that colleges and universities might have to re-evaluate their academic outcomes in terms of post-college student be-haviors in a reappraisal of the central role traditionally assigned academic talent.

Summary of Research on Impact

Colleges and universities do have a significant impact upon the attitudes and values of their students. The changes that have been occurring with considerable consistency in recent decades include declining au-thoritarianism, dogmatism, and prejudice, decreasing conservative at-titudes, and growing sensitivity to aesthetic experiences. These changes appear to take place in all types of institutions, although the degree and nature of the impact of different colleges vary with the characteristics of the entering students. The impact of the institution is very likely to accentuate the strengths and interests of individuals who select it for its particular character or reputation. Faculty members are often influential in intellec-tual matters and in career decisions, but do not appear to be responsible for institutionwide impact except in settings where the influence of student peers and faculty complement and reinforce one another. The influence of residence and peer groups upon students' attitudes and values appears to be quite strong, especially in the small, four-year colleges where there is a fairly high degree of homogeneity among students and faculty. Changes that take place in attitudes and values among college students also take place among non-college attenders of the same age, but to a much greater extent among the college attenders. Attitudes held by college students tend to persist for many years after college, especially when the graduates live in a social environment that supports these attitudes. The impact of college achievement upon significant adult accomplishment is not very striking. It appears that success in the various occupations that college graduates enter is relatively independent of academic performance in college.

Implications of Research on College Impact

College administrators and faculty need to become aware of the kinds of impacts their institutions have and do not have. Too often, assumptions are made in the planning and retention of educational programs and policies that are not supported by any kind of evidence. Some educational leaders may not agree that it is the institution's "business" to be concerned about the attitudes and values of its students. Others may be convinced that the traditional academic program has wide applicability and transference value for its graduates despite existing evidence to the contrary. Individual departments may need to be convinced that it is necessary to plan academic programs jointly with other departments if there is going to be much coherence perceived by the undergraduates. The student personnel staff may need to be persuaded to join with the faculty in attempts to create closer ties between students and staff, especially in informal settings. The residence and peer group arrangements on and off campus may need to be studied to see if there are ways to make the experience of students more educational.

The institution must decide what its priorities and goals are within its role and scope. It cannot be "all things to all students," but it can have a significant and important impact upon students within its limitations.

The research on impact of colleges clearly indicates that enough is known about the conditions of impact so that an institution should not merely leave such matters to chance. It can and it should decide consciously about the type of institution that it can realistically be—the students it can attract, the curriculum it can offer, the social environment it can provide, and the particular character it wants to portray. Overall, the institution must become aware of its campus as a learning environment, where all its components interact in special ways to comprise a set of educational experiences for its students. These do not simply consist of a few hours each week in classrooms, but are an accumulation of social, personal, academic, religious, athletic, vocational, political, and aesthetic experiences that together comprise the impact of the college.

The institution may have to review its priorities regarding the importance traditionally assigned to academic skills, and consider additional talents among its students that should be encouraged and rewarded. The research on impact reveals that much of the change that takes place among undergraduates occurs in the first two years of college. Such information might serve as a stimulus for institutions to develop new educational experiences in the last two years of college so that they might also be meaningful for students in terms of their continuing growth. Colleges and universities, especially large ones, may want to consider new organizational arrangements of their campuses, to maximize the possibilities of impacts by creating smaller, more homogeneous subgroups of students and faculty that can interact in more personal ways. All these implications of college impact studies imply some form of change within institutions. The process of change is not an easy one for most colleges and universities, especially when basic policies and traditional assumptions are challenged. It is clear, however, that if existing institutions are to maximize their impacts upon students, their programs and priorities must undergo a considerable amount of adjustment.

References

Allport, G.W., Vernon, P.E., and Lindzey, G. *Manual, Study of Values*. Boston: Houghton Mifflin. 1960, 1970.

Astin, Alexander W. *The College Environment*. Washington, D.C.: American Council on Education. 1968a.

————. "Undergraduate Achievement and Institutional Excellence." *Science*. 1968b. Vol. 161, 661-668.

————. "The Impact of Dormitory Living on Students." *Educational Record*. Summer 1973. pp. 204- 210.

————, and Panos, Robert J. *The Educational and Vocational Development of College Students*. Washington, D.C.: American Council on Education. 1969.

Bayer, A.E., Royer, J.T., and Webb, R.M. *Four Years after College Entry*. Washington, D.C.: American Council on Education Research Reports, vol. 8, no. 1. 1973.

Bushnell, John H. "Student Culture at Vassar." In Sanford, Nevitt, *The American College*. New York: John Wiley and Sons, 1962.

Chickering, A.W. *Education and Identity*. San Francisco: Jossey-Bass. 1969, p. 278. Reprinted with permission.

————. "College Experience and Student Development," Speech given at the meeting of the American Association for the Advancement of Science. 1970.

————. "The Best Colleges Have the Least Effect." *Saturday Review*. 1971. Vol. 54, no. 3, 48-50.

————. *Commuting Versus Resident Students*. San Francisco: Jossey-Bass, 1974.

————, et al. *Research and Action: Third Annual Progress Report Covering the Period from April 1965 through December 31, 1967*. Plainfield, Vt.: Project on Student Development in Small Colleges. 1968.

Clark, Burton. "The Culture of the College: Its Implications for the Organization of Learning Resources." Paper presented at the Conference on the Library and the College Climate of Learning, Syracuse University, June 1965.

Dressel, P.L., and Lehmann, I.J. "The Impact of Higher Education on Student Attitudes, Values, and Critical Thinking Abilities." *Educational Record*. Summer 1965. Vol. 46, no. 3, 248-258.

————, and Mayhew, L.B. *General Education: Explorations in Evaluation*. Washington, D.C.: American Council on Education. 1954.

Feldman, Kenneth A. *College and Student: Selected Readings in the*

Social Psychology of Higher Education. New York: Pergamon Press. 1972.

———, and Newcomb, T.M. *The Impact of College on Students*. San Francisco: Jossey-Bass, 1969, p. 333.

Freedman, Mervin B. *The College Experience*. San Francisco: Jossey-Bass, 1967.

———, and Bereiter, C. "A Longitudinal Study of Personality Development in College Alumnae." *Merrill-Palmer Quarterly of Behavior and Development*. 1963. Vol. 9, 295-301.

Grigg, C.M. "Recruitment to Graduate Study: College Seniors' Plans for Postgraduate Education and Their Implementation the Year after Commencement." SREB Research Monograph No. 10. Atlanta, Ga.: Southern Regional Education Board. 1965.

Gurin, Gerald. "The Impact of the College Experience." In Withey, S.B., *A Degree and What Else? Correlates and Consequences of a College Education*. New York: McGraw-Hill, 1971.

Gurin, G., and Katz, D. "Motivation and Aspiration in the Negro College." Office of Education, U.S. Department of HEW. Project No. 5-0787. Ann Arbor, Mich.: Survey Research Center, Institution for Social Research, University of Michigan, 1966.

Heath, D.H. *Growing Up in College*. San Francisco: Jossey-Bass, 1968.

Hodgkinson, Harold. "Higher Education and the Aged." Speech given at the Conference sponsored by the Center for Gerontogical Studies, University of Florida. Gainesville, Fla. April 8, 1975.

Hoyt, D.P. "The Relationship between College Grads and Adult Achievement: A Review of the Literature." A.C.T. Research Report No. 7. Iowa City, Iowa: The American College Testing Program, 1965.

———. "The Impact of Student Personnel Work on Student Development." Address delivered to the 1966 Conference of the Kansas Association of Student Personnel Administrators, Rock Springs, Kans.: October 9, 1966.

Huntley, C.W. "Changes in Study of Value Scores during the Four Years of College." *Genetic Psychology Monographs*. 1965. Vol. 71, 349-383.

Jacob, P.E. *Changing Values in College: An Exploratory Study of the Impact of College Teaching*. New York: Harper. 1957.

Katz, Joseph, and Associates. *No Time for Youth: Growth and Constraint in College Students*. San Francisco: Jossey-Bass, 1969.

Kerr, Clark. Quoted in the Foreward of Withey, Stephen B., *A Degree and What Else? Correlates and Consequences of a College Education*. New York: McGraw-Hill. 1971.

Korn, Harold A. "Personality Scale Changes from the Freshman Year to the Senior Year." In Katz, Joseph (Ed.), *No Time for Youth: Growth and Constraint in College Students*. San Francisco: Jossey-Bass. 1968.

Lehmann, Irving J. "Changes in Critical Thinking, Attitudes and Values from Freshman to Senior Years." *Journal of Educational Psychology*, 1963. Vol. 54, 312.

Lenning, O.T., Munday, L.A., and Maxey, E.J. "Student Educational Growth during the First Two Years of College." *College and University*. 1969. Vol. 44, 145-153.

Lozoff, Marjorie M. "Residential Groups and Individual Development." In Katz, Joseph, and Associates. *No Time for Youth: Growth and Constraint in College Students*. San Francisco: Jossey-Bass. 1969

McConnell, T.R. "Differences in Student Attitudes toward Civil Liberties." In Sutherland R.L., et al. (Eds.) *Personality Factors on the College Campus: Review of a Symposium*. Austin, Tex.: The Hogg Foundation for Mental Health. 1962.

Miller, Eleanor O. "Nonacademic Changes in College Students." *Educational Record*. 1959. Vol. 40, 118-122.

Munday, L.A., and Davis, J.C. "Varieties of Accomplishment after College: Perspectives on the Meaning of Academic Talent." A.C.T. Research Report No. 62. Iowa City, Iowa: The American College Testing Program, 1974.

Newcomb, T.M. *Personality and Social Change: Attitude Formation in a Student Community*. New York: Holt. 1943.

————. "Student Peer-Group Influence." In Sanford, Nevitt, *The American College*. New York: John Wiley & Sons, 1962.

————, Koenig, K.E., Flacks, R., and Warwick, D.P. *Persistence and Change: Bennington College and Its Students after Twenty-five Years*. New York: John Wiley & Sons. 1967.

————, and Wilson, E.K. (Eds.) *College Peer Groups: Problems and Prospects for Research*. Chicago: Aldine. 1966.

Pace, C.R., and Stern, G.G. "An Approach to the Measurement of Psychological Characteristics of College Environments." *Journal of Educational Psychology*. 1958. Vol. 49, 269-277.

Plant, Walter T. "Personality Changes Associated with a College Education." U.S. Department of HEW. Cooperative Research Branch Project 348. San Jose State College, San Jose Calif. 1962.

————. "Longitudinal Changes in Intolerance and Authoritarianism for Subjects Differing in Amount of Education over Four Years." *Genetic Psychology Monograph*, 1965, Vol. 72, 247-287.

Raushenbush, E. *The Student and His Studies*. Middletown, Conn.: Wesleyan University Press, 1964, p. 86.

Richards, J.M., Holland, J.L., and Lutz, S.W. The Assessment of Student Accomplishment in College. ACT Research Report No. 11, Iowa City, Iowa: The American College Testing Program, 1966.

Riesman, David. "The Jacob Report." *American Sociological Review*. 1958. Vol. 23, 732-738.

Riley, J.W., Ryan, B.F., and Lifshitz, M. *The Student Looks at His Teacher: An Inquiry Into the Implications of Student Ratings at the College Level*. New Brunswick, N.J.: Rutgers University Press. 1950.

Sanford, Nevitt. "Personality Development during the College Years." *Personnel and Guidance Journal*. 1956. Vol. 35, 74-80.

_____. *The American College*. New York: John Wiley & Sons. 1962.

_____. *Where Colleges Fail*. San Francisco: Jossey-Bass. 1967.

Smith, G.H. "Liberalism and Level of Information." *Journal of Educational Psychology*. 1948. Vol. 39, 65-81.

Spaights, E. "Students Appraise Teachers' Methods and Attitudes." *Improving College and University Teaching*. 1967. Vol. 15, 15-17.

Trent, J.W., and Medsker, L.L. *Beyond High School: A Psychological Study of 10,000 High School Graduates*. San Francisco: Jossey-Bass, 1968.

Underwood, K. Personal communication and preliminary manuscripts for *The Church, The University, and Social Policy*. Report of the Director, The Danforth Study of Campus Ministries, 1968.

Wallace, W.L. *Student Culture: Social Structure and Continuity in a Liberal Arts College*. Chicago: Aldine, 1966.

Webster, H., Freedman, M., and Heist, P. "Personality Changes in College Students." In Sanford, Nevitt, *The American College*. New York: John Wiley & Sons, 1962.

Wilson, W. "The Spirit of Learning" (1909). In *Selected Literary and Political Papers and Addresses of Woodrow Wilson*, Vol. 1, New York: Grosset and Dunlap, 1925, p. 244.

Withey, Stephen B. *A Degree and What Else? Correlates and Consequences of a College Education*. New York: McGraw-Hill, 1971, p. 129.

5

An Institution That Can Affect Students: A Case Description

In the first four chapters of this book, background was provided about the crisis in undergraduate education, and the literature was reviewed regarding the characteristics and problems of students. The impacts that institutions have upon students and the conditions under which these impacts occur were also described. Undergraduate education is in a state of crisis. Although there are many innovative programs being initiated currently, too often they are isolated from the total curriculum and do not represent campuswide reform. The "curriculum" for many undergraduates reflects the priorities of individual departments more than a coherent set of educational objectives. While much of current teaching is effective and new approaches are being tried, too often undergraduate teaching, especially for first- and second-year students, is not viewed as a high priority for faculty. At the larger universities in particular, where graduate programs claim much of the prestige, resources, and rewards, the undergraduate experience is often impersonal and frustrating. Students are too likely to be left to their own devices in such crucial areas as academic advising and the choice of a major or career that fits their needs. While it is evident that students often change their attitudes and values in college, most changes take place not in response to any conscious effort on the part of the institution, but because of the motivation process itself and the interaction of students with others who already share their point of view. There have been significant changes in the kinds of students entering colleges and universities in recent years, but there have not been corresponding changes in the academic and student services offered. The current economy has brought faculty mobility to a virtual standstill; in turn, this has made it more likely that institutions will be staffed by faculty who are not regularly stimulated by the influx of new and younger colleagues. It also appears that existing faculty may "hang on" to their current positions (more often tenured than not) as survival takes first priority, and the "generation gap" that exists among some students and faculty may widen. The growing interest among faculty in collective bargaining may further complicate the current situation in undergraduate education, and it may make efforts at reform even more difficult. As a result, faculty may focus more on their own power and rights, and less on the institutionwide needs of the students. Finally, the financial crunch being experienced by many institutions now may cause some colleges to resort to academic "gimickry" in their efforts

95

to recruit and retain undergraduates. Such actions, while they may gain some short-lived publicity, have little intellectual substance, do not represent a coherent educational point of view, and cheat the undergraduates they are intended to serve.

There are, of course, many more problems in undergraduate education than have been listed here. There has been some encouraging evidence recently that there is real interest in addressing these problems. Bell (1966), Martin (1968), Gaff (1970), Levine and Weingart (1973), and *Change* Magazine (1974) are the most notable examples. There is a need for institutional models, for campuswide programs that reflect a coherent set of objectives. While many undergraduates at various institutions enjoy highly effective educational experiences, these still are too often a function of personality, geographical accident, or good fortune. The "pockets of excellence" that exist on most campuses (especially large ones) often function in spite of the rest of the institution, and only a few "lucky" students are able to benefit from them.

It is assumed in this chapter that there is an urgent need for change in undergraduate education, and that models of undergraduate programs are needed that go beyond piecemeal reforms. The purpose of the chapter is to present one case description of an institutional program designed to affect students in defined ways. It is not being suggested that this model is appropriate for all institutions or for all students. Rather, it is one hypothetical example of an institution's efforts to provide effective educational programs to its students within the context of its mission.

Segar University

Overview

Segar University is a state-supported institution located in Gullander, a Midwestern city with a population of about 80,000. Its current enrollment is 3,600, entirely undergraduate. The university was founded in 1938; it experienced its greatest enrollment growth in the 1960s, increasing from 2,000 students in 1962 to 3,800 students in 1969. Its enrollment has now leveled off, and is expected to remain at about 3,600 for the next several years.

Segar has had its own board of trustees since its founding. The eighteen-member board consists of three citizens of the state appointed by the state's governor, three nationally prominent educators (neither residents of the state nor graduates of Segar), three members of the city of Gullander elected every six years by the community, three graduates of

Segar elected every six years by the members of the alumni association, three faculty elected by the faculty every six years, and three students elected by the students every two years. The governor of the state appoints the chairperson of the board from three state appointees. The board meets four times per year; it has a strong tradition of supporting the autonomy of the university, and its president can make decisions within the broad policy guidelines of the board itself. The president of Segar University is an ex-officio member of the board, and, of course, is appointed by them. In its 37-year history, Segar has had five presidents, and since 1965, the board has decided that presidents should not serve more than seven years. Its current president, Everett Reier, was appointed in 1971.

Objectives of Segar University

Although there have been changes in the stated objectives of Segar over the years, the fundamental commitments of the institution have remained stable. The university has established a reputation for vigorous academic programs, good teaching, service to society, and international understanding. These primary emphases have been evident since the university's founding and have been reflected throughout its programs. The board of trustees plays a major but not exclusive role in the determination of these institutional objectives, and it holds the president accountable for them.

The objectives of Segar University are as follows.

Segar University is a state-supported institution, founded in 1938. It strives, through its various educational programs, to emphasize high quality in its teaching and curriculum, international understanding, and service to society. It seeks students and faculty who are willing to work together with members of the community toward these goals. Specifically, these are the outcomes that Segar University is seeking to realize in its students:

(1) *Intellectual competence*. Students should be able to demonstrate a significant level of expertise in an academic area of concentration as well as a basic knowledge of general education.

(2) *International understanding*. Students should be knowledgeable about and sensitive to a wide variety of world cultures, and should give evidence of this knowledge by their increased awareness of the world as a community.

(3) *Service to society*. Students should become aware of their personal responsibility to others and should express this commitment by visible and concrete service to their community.

(4) *A sense of values*. Students should become aware of their own value priorities and their origin, as well as the implications for their lives. The university strives to help students become less ethnocentric and authori-

tarian in their thinking, and more appreciative and understanding of others who represent diverse viewpoints.

(5) *A sense of confidence*. The university strives to assist students to become autonomous, independent persons who have a sense of confidence in their interactions with people, ideas, and work.

(6) *Facility of expression*. The university strives to help students become more effective in expressing themselves in writing and in speaking. Students should be able to present their ideas clearly to others and to engage in mutual problem-solving efforts with others.

Segar University is deeply committed to the education of its students and recognizes that the period of four undergraduate years is only a beginning for a life-long learning commitment. It will consider its educational program successful to the extent that the actual postcollege activities and accomplishments of its greduates reflect the goals and objectives of the university. Finally, it expects that students will not cease their commitment to nor participation in the affairs of Segar after they have graduated. To a considerable extent, the success of this educational community depends upon the continuing concern of its graduates.

Instead of commenting further on these objectives at this point, a description of the university's organizational structure and educational program, which reflect these objectives, will be presented.

Organizational Structure and Governance

Segar is organized in a manner that reflects its emphases as an institution. It stresses a strong sense of participation by the members of the university; it also strives to develop primary responsibility for programs in a decentralized fashion, whereby students and faculty sharing similar interests are known to each other. Its organizational structure is intended to encourage diversity, not uniformity, and open discussion and debate, not rules and regulations. That different "standards" may exist at the university among its colleges is considered an asset rather than an inconsistency. Controversy and vigorous debate on educational objectives, programs, and issues not only are encouraged, but are a constant and necessary condition of the organizational structure. The lively and sometimes vehement arguments that take place at the Segar University Assembly (SUA) meetings are a campus tradition that students and faculty relish.

The president of Segar is the chief administrative officer of the institution and is responsible to the board of trustees, which was described earlier. While the president speaks for the University to the trustees, the faculty and students have a major role in decisionmaking through the Segar University Assembly (SUA) and a number of intracollege and intercollege committees. Although the board of trustees actually hires the president, the faculty and students of Segar assume the major responsibility in the search and screening process. While the president occupies a position of considerable influence, his/her power is expressed most frequently and effectively through persuasion and by actual participation in the life of the university. All administrators at Segar, including the president, teach in one of the colleges, and the president also serves as the Chairperson of the Segar University Assembly. As can be seen in the organizational chart (Figure 5-1), the Assembly constitutes the major legislative body of the university. (Also see the map in Figure 5-2.)

The Assembly consists of the three college deans, three other administrators (the Coordinator of International Programs, the Coordinator of Student Advising Programs, and the Director of Business Affairs), fifteen faculty members (five elected from each of the three colleges), and fifteen student members (five elected from each of the three colleges). The president chairs the Assembly which meets once per month, or more often depending upon the need. The president may call a special meeting, or a minimum of twelve members of the Assembly (one-third) may also call it together. The Assembly is the oldest tradition at Segar, having been created by its first president. There is lively competition each year among students and faculty to become elected to the Assembly, and each of the colleges determines its own method of election. In one college, for example, a student member of each class must be represented, and faculty representation must reflect different areas of academic concentration. In another college, the elections are "wide open," and students and faculty vote in elections for both groups.

All the universitywide committees are responsible to the Assembly. At the present time, there are fifteen committees of this kind, which, among others, include budget, physical facilities, student advising, institutional studies, international programs, and staff benefits. When a universitywide committee has a proposal for a new program or a policy change, it presents the proposal to the Assembly. After debate and discussion, the Assembly votes on such proposals, and their action is formally sent to the University president, who either accepts or rejects them. While the president has this final veto, he has only used it in rare situations over the years. As Chairperson of the Assembly, the president is an active participant in the process of discussion, so that her or his point of view on most matters is evident to faculty and students. Although any other member of the Segar University community may bring matters directly to the attention of the Assembly, most often the initial work and discussion on issues and problems takes place in either the universitywide committees or the individual colleges.

It is highly significant to note that there has never existed at Segar a formal, separate faculty or student government. The structure of commit-

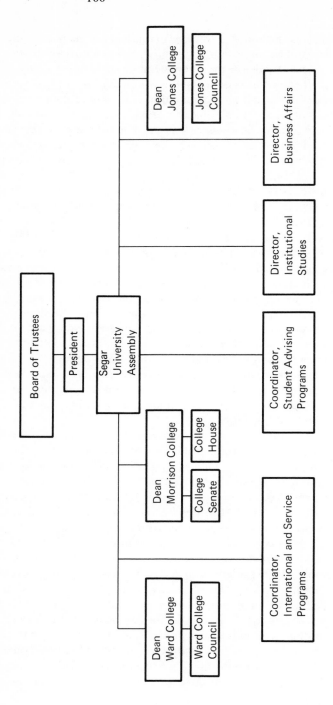

Figure 5-1. Segar University Organizational Chart, 1975.

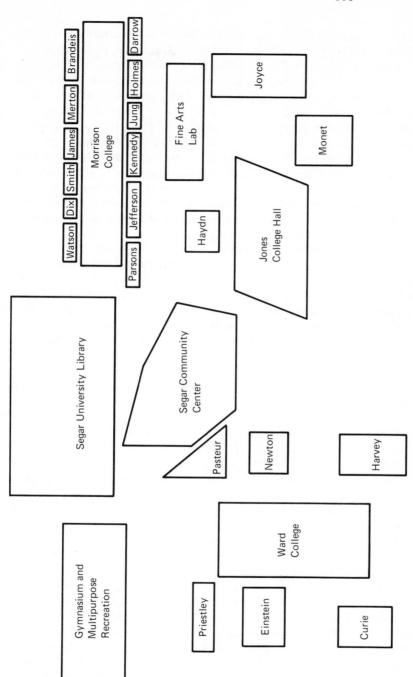

Figure 5-2. Segar University Map, 1975.

tees and the Assembly have been viewed, since the university's founding, as effective vehicles for involvement in the decision-making process. Students are represented with a vote on the Assembly in equal numbers with the faculty, and are also full participants on the universitywide committees. There have been minor changes in this structure over the years (for example, the size of the Assembly has fluctuated), but the fundamental nature of the system has remained intact. For students and faculty, it is a matter of considerable status (and hard work) to be elected to the Assembly. During the period from 1968 to 1972, when protests concerning the Vietnam conflict were so prevalent, the Assembly faced one of its most difficult challenges from students. Although there were emotionally heated debates frequently in the Assembly on the appropriate response of the institution to the war, many students disagreed with the refusal of the Assembly to take a particular political stand on the "immorality of the war," as students called it. This eventually resulted in a walkout of most of the student representatives (and some of the faculty), and the "Segar People's Council" was formed as a response. This ad hoc group existed for less than a year. It made public a number of its concerns, but its members eventually saw that they could not have the impact they desired, and they dissolved the group. There still are some bitter feelings among students and faculty on the role of the institution in face of such crises as the Vietnam War, but they are debated formally in the Assembly.

The legislature of the state, faced with decreasing revenues and increasing aspirations for higher education, has not been able to meet all the budget requests and needs of Segar during the past two years. This has resulted in some dissatisfaction among the faculty, whose salaries are not as competitive with other institutions as they once were. There is currently some discussion among the faculty about collective bargaining as a method to regain some of their lost economic benefits. When the issue came to the floor of the Assembly for the first time eight months ago, there resulted one of the most heated debates anyone can remember. The Segar community is greatly concerned about this matter now, and the eventual outcome could have a major effect upon the Assembly and upon the entire governance structure of the institution.

Although the role of the Segar University Assembly is highly significant in the governance process, all members of the university would agree that the primary focus of decisionmaking, planning, and program development takes place within each of the colleges. Although the colleges are described in greater detail later in this chapter, especially in regard to their academic programs, their role in the governance structure is discussed here.

From its beginning, Segar University has been committed to the "cluster college" concept, whereby individual colleges, relatively small in size, have been created around particular academic concentrations. While students enroll in one of the colleges and identify with it and live within its residential units, they take courses in the other colleges as well, according to their needs. Faculty members have their assignments within individual colleges, but more freely from one to another as well.

The governance structure of each college is different, and reflects both the diversity of points of view at Segar, and the highly prized autonomy of the colleges. Ward College, with its primary emphasis in the physical and biological sciences, has a fairly traditional structure of committees among its four divisions, and has the Ward College Council as its main decision-making group. The council is patterned after the Segar University Assembly, and is composed of students and faculty of the college, with the Dean serving as Chairperson. Since almost all the usual university functions are decentralized into the colleges, there is a great deal of significance for the faculty and students to do. Admissions, financial aid, teaching assignments, promotions, salary adjustments, curriculum decisions—all these matters are decided by the college itself, and they may or may not conform to the methods used or specific policies followed by the other colleges. Thus, there is a very strong identification with each of the colleges on the part of the faculty and students; they play a major role because not only do they determine the content and structure of the college's program, but they also retain the responsibility for its performance and outcomes. Ward College is the newest of the colleges at Segar, having been started in 1947. Its College Council has not had the lengthy debates so characteristic of the other colleges, as most of the issues become resolved in the college committees, among the four college divisions. For example, four years ago, the admissions committee of the college struggled for several weeks over a proposed revision of its policy which would result in more active recruitment of minority students. While there was little resistance to the concept itself, the policy change could have implications for other areas of college concern, such as advising, curriculum, and financial aid. When these matters were eventually resolved within the college committees to the satisfaction of the students and faculty, the matter was acted upon after less than an hour's discussion by the Ward College Council. Of the three colleges, Ward has had the most stable and predictable governance structure in the past several years. Although its students and faculty resist any kind of stereotyping, students in the other colleges enjoy declaring that Ward is "overly structured, conservative, and straight." Such friendly perceptions are given vigorous expression in the various intercollege athletic events held throughout the year.

Jones College has existed since the founding of Segar, and its primary emphasis is in the humanities and fine arts. It takes considerable pride in what it considers to be its rigorous curriculum, in the large number of its graduates who go on to professional schools, and especially in its "Jones

Town Council." The "JTC," as it has been called for years, is the major governance unit for the college, and it closely resembles the "town meeting" concept in early American history. Although there are several college committees which have (at least on paper!) a significant role in college affairs, everyone in the college is aware that the real "action" takes place at the JTC. These meetings are held every month, or when at least 15 percent of the college members (students and faculty) sign a petition asking for a meeting. Although the JTC amazingly operates without a formal constitution, it has developed, over the years, a well-understood set of "common laws" that govern its meetings. No student or faculty member is unaware, for example, that at least 70 members of the college need to be present for a meeting to be "legal," or that it takes action by two consecutive meetings of the JTC on an issue before the matter can go to the dean for approval. However, these "rules" are not written down anywhere, and any attempt to do so would be viewed as heresy within the college. The debates in the JTC are legendary, and often have to be held in the Segar Community Center, the largest hall on campus. Often they attract students and faculty from the other colleges as observers, a matter of no small pride to the Jones community. What is regarded as utter chaos in college governance by outsiders (such as the Ward College faculty) is viewed with beauty and pride by the Jones academic community. A visitor once remarked that she had no idea how decisions were made in Jones College after having observed them for a month, but admitted with obvious envy that somehow they "get the job done" and have a reputation for excellence and innovation! Jones has always prized participation and the free expression of ideas over any kind of formal structure. While emotions often become heated in the endless discussions and debates at the college, it is noteworthy that students identify strongly with the college and its program, even after graduation. Jones has had the highest rate of alumni donations each year since its founding, as its graduates remain actively interested in the college's future.

Morrison College was also begun when Segar was founded, and its primary emphasis lies in the social and behavioral sciences. Its governance structure is based upon a legislative bicameral model. Thus, there are two primary groups that can take action on various college issues, and policies: the Morrison College Senate (MCS) and the Morrison College House (MCH). Before a recommendation can be sent to the college dean for approval, positive action is required by both the MCS and the MCH. In striking contrast to the informal, ad hoc nature of Jones College, Morrison has an extensive college constitution, which includes specific rules and procedures for the consideration of policy matters. Formal "bills" are presented at the MCS meetings by the elected student and faculty senators, and at the MCH meetings by the elected student and faculty representatives. Conference committees exist to resolve differences in bills before the two bodies, much as they are in Congress. Each group has its own elected chairperson (who, at times, has been a student), and when the two bodies meet occasionally in joint session, the Morrison College dean presides. Each body has a set of committees, although in recent years many of these committees have become joint senate-house units. The roles of the college dean, the senators, representatives, and committee chairpersons are well defined in the college constitution. Since many of the Morrison College graduates have attended law school after graduation in past years, the other colleges at Segar delight in teasing members of Morrison about the long hours spent on debate over "trivial legal issues." Members of Morrison College are strongly committed to what they consider the "most logical, and only truly rational" way of running a college at Segar. Although identification with one's college is strong—and this is reflected in the comments made frequently about the other colleges—most often these comments are made in good humor among friends, and indicate a respect for another college's right to "do its own thing." Morrison's curricular emphasis upon the social and behavioral sciences is reflected in its high participation in community service programs. One of the matters that the MCS and MCH worked on during the past year at considerable length was a proposal to increase the amount of community service for academic credit required in the college during the sophomore and junior years.

Although the colleges are largely autonomous, their major policies and programs need final approval, in most cases, by the Segar University Assembly. The Assembly has been very cautious over the years about "invading" the autonomy of the colleges, but vigorously rejects any suggestions that it is a "rubber-stamp" organization for them. As mentioned before, the Assembly has fifteen standing universitywide committees that are responsible to it, and each of these has considerable influence upon the colleges and their faculty and students. Perhaps the most significant of these (especially as viewed by the deans!) is the universitywide budget committee of the Assembly. It has the responsibility for hearing proposals by the college deans each year concerning their total budgetary needs, and then it submits recommendations to the total Assembly for final action. The college deans develop their budget proposals in accordance with their own college's governance structure, and in cooperation with the university's director of business affairs. While the deans are in no way restricted from going to the president of Segar regarding their budget, both tradition and the process itself operate against such "individual and unilateral" actions. Some outside observers have commented that such a governance structure makes leadership difficult for the deans and the president, and in almost all cases, the deans and the president would agree. However, they remain committed to the diverse, and largely democratic, system of decisionmaking, and on most occasions claim that the existing structure encourages much more openness and confidence in the decisions, once they are made. They also agree that this structure demands a more complex style of leadership—one based on persuasion, sound proposals, and statesmanship, rather than on power, money, or favored personal relationships. Perhaps most important at Segar, the governance process is supportive of and consistent with the educational objectives to which the institution is committed for its students. Segar understands that among the most important conditions of impact are such things as close identification with faculty in a college that is committed to a set of ideals, and a sense of shared responsibility for the success of the venture. The governance structure further enhances the institution's objectives by providing frequent and meaningful participation by students in the process, whereby they learn to express themselves and their ideas in realistic settings. The lively diversity that exists in the governance process supports the kinds of values and attitudes Segar desires in its graduates. Finally, the opportunity for student involvement in governance provides an ideal setting for them to test out their ideas and their abilities, thus contributing to the sense of confidence the institution strives to encourage in its students.

The governance process at Segar, with all its traditions, diversity, and good fellowship, is not an end in itself, but is recognized as only a means to the end of realizing the university's objectives. It has changed over the years, and will undoubtedly continue to change as new programs are developed, new faculty and students come to the campus, and needs change. However, governance is rarely viewed as "red tape" at Segar, because most recognize its significant role as part of the educational program itself. The constant proposals to alter some policy or program, or to raise new questions about educational issues, are viewed as a positive symbol of the institution's health, not an indication of its weakness or instability. As one faculty member commented, "What I love most about this place is that nothing is ever settled—if it were, it would cease to be Segar." The faculty has recognized that this continual "turmoil" can be frustrating for undergraduates, who often are looking for final answers. Indeed, the university is always trying to maintain a healthy balance between "contentment and irritation" in students, realizing that some disorientation is probably necessary for the most effective learning to take place, while too much can operate at cross purposes with its objectives.

The Colleges

Although Segar University has attained a national reputation over the years, it is best known for its three colleges—Ward, Jones, and Morrison. From its founding, Segar has been committed to the cluster-college concept. Each college is a semiautonomous residential and academic unit that serves the needs of its students and faculty in a personal way. While retaining the benefits of smallness, the cluster concept also enjoys the benefits of largeness, as students and faculty can move freely about the other colleges and make use of the excellent facilities and programs that can only be present with adequate size. Segar has never made any claim that this is a new or innovative arrangement, and has openly borrowed frequently from such programs as Santa Cruz, New College, Justin Morrill, and Raymond. Segar has its major emphasis upon undergraduate education, and is strongly committed to the cluster concept as the best method of providing a diverse range of opportunities to students as well as an effective and personal academic program.

Although the colleges are semiautonomous and actually occupy separate physical and residential facilities, they share the Segar University Library, several administrative services (such as purchasing), and the Segar Community Center. The Center was built in the late 1940s so that students, faculty, and community members might come together more often for a variety of activites. The Center includes an informal cafeteria, a pub, many small meeting rooms, a theatre-auditorium, recreational and athletic facilities, art display areas, music listening rooms, and some administrative offices. The Community Center (the "C-C" as it is known at Segar) is the hub of activity on the campus, and virtually never closes. It is the center for social, recreational, and cultural programs. Almost everyone at Segar is there at least once per day for one reason or another; and, of course, that is the intent of the multipurpose facility. Most students feel that "things aren't so dull at Segar, because there's always something going on at the C-C."

Segar experimented with some graduate programs in 1964, offering them in three areas on a universitywide basis. Although the faculty were, for the most part, in favor of the experiment when it was initiated, the graduate programs were discontinued in 1967 because it was felt by all three of the colleges that the graduate programs could interfere with undergraduate priorities as defined by Segar. This was a difficult and major decision for the university which made some faculty quite unhappy. For the majority, however, the decision reaffirmed the commitment of Segar to its primary mission. As the president stated in his address to the Assembly, "The discontinuation of our graduate programs is not an indication of our lack of flexibility, or our inability to develop high-quality graduate education; rather, it is a positive statement by this academic community that we have discovered again our primary mission, and that we should do nothing that might detract from it." In future years, perhaps, a proposal may be made again for graduate programs; but at the present time there is little discussion of it.

Each of the colleges is governed by the same academic calendar, although there are almost constant debates at Segar about the best or most appropriate calendar for the campus. The calendar now followed is the "4-4-2" plan, as Segar calls it. The first semester begins on September 1 and concludes on December 20. The second semester begins on January 15 and concludes on May 7. The third segment, called simply the "term," begins on June 1 and concludes on July 25. Although "regular" courses can be taken during the "term," it is mainly a period for independent study, field work, cooperative education, and special academic projects. Only about half of the faculty are on the payroll during this period. Segar has made considerable progress in the past ten years in increasing the enrollment during the "term," but no more than half of the students have enrolled in any one "term." All are required, however, to enroll for at least one "term" during their four years at Segar. Proposals have been made for virtually every kind of academic calendar imaginable, but the current one will probably persist for the next several years.

Although they will be described in more detail later, the relationships of the colleges to three universitywide offices (see Figure 5-1) should be noted briefly here.

All Segar students are required to participate in an international experience and a service program during their undergraduate years. Although the colleges retain responsibility for determining the appropriate kinds of experiences students should have, and when they should have them, coordination is provided by a central office. Through this office, many of the mechanical details are handled, and needed coordination with the other colleges at Segar (and with other institutions) is accomplished.

Although academic advising is also primarily a college activity, there is the Segar Advising Center, which provides coordination for the overall program as well as personnel for the many interviews that students have as part of their undergraduate experience. The colleges maintain close contact with the Advising Center, which is viewed as an integral part of the educational program at Segar.

The Institutional Studies Office at Segar, while responsible to the president (through the Assembly), works closely with the colleges in their attempts to learn more about their students, the impact of their programs, and the educational needs of the community. The Institutional Studies Office is often quite influential in the planning of new programs, and in the development of new policies at Segar. A description of each of the three colleges follows.

Ward College. Ward College, with its emphasis in the physical and biological sciences, was founded in 1947. It was known simply as "college three" for two years, when the trustees named it for John Ward, a distinguished chemist and faculty member at Segar who originally proposed the idea for the college, and served as chairperson of the "Commission on College Three." Professor Ward retired from Segar in 1950 at age 70, but served as a consultant for several years after that time. From the beginning, the basic purpose of Ward College has been to link science with humans. Convinced that science cannot be merely an impersonal, valuefree technology existing apart from the lives of human beings, the college was created to educate "humanistic scientists," who could use science for the betterment of people. The founders of Ward College had been greatly affected by the events of World War II, and especially by the use of the advanced technology as represented by the atomic bomb. In 1946, Professor Ward was concerned about the kinds of scientific development that might take place in future years, and, especially, in the kinds of people that our colleges would matriculate in the various scientific disciplines. While insisting on a rigorous and sophisticated education in the physical and biological sciences, Professor Ward saw an equal need for undergraduates to become aware of human problems that science might address, and the human implications of scientific decisions. These basic convictions have remained as the foundation for Ward College, and they are reflected in its entire program.

Students enter Ward College in their first year, but do not have to choose an area of concentration until the beginning of their third year. Although there is extensive flexibility in the curriculum, so that a student can arrange a "college contract" with his/her advising committee, all students in Ward take considerable amounts of chemistry, physics, mathematics, biology, and philosophy of science. Some of the course work in these areas is taught in cooperation with faculty members from Jones and Morrison Colleges, especially in the junior and senior years. "Science and Man," "The Ethical Implications of Science," "Biology and Public Policy," and "Technology and Its Impact on Personality" are examples of courses that are team-taught by faculty from Ward and the other colleges.

Ward students are also required to take at least one-fourth of their undergraduate program in an area of the humanities or social sciences. They are given considerable flexibility to select electives during their four years, as long as these electives can be "justified" to their advising committee. Each Ward College student (this is true for all three colleges) is assigned a three-person advising committee upon entrance. This committee includes a staff member from the Segar Advising Center (usually a counseling psychologist), a faculty member from Ward from an academic area in which the student has indicated an interest, and another faculty member from an area quite divergent from the student's stated interest. This committee, chaired by the faculty member representing the student's area of academic interest, meets formally with the student at least twice per year, in structured efforts to assist in his or her development. The committee has the authority (within college guidelines) to approve the entire academic program for the student, to evaluate the student's progress (or lack of it), and to require various educational experiences for the student. The same three faculty meet with the student for four years, unless the student requests a change, or unless the student changes his or her academic concentration or college. The student and the advising committee eventually arrive at a ''college contract'' which represents the agreed-upon program of study the student will follow. The advising committee is intended to be among the major educational experiences in the undergraduate program, and it includes a set of fairly structured interviews over the four years. These will be described later in more detail.

During their undergraduate program, the students in Ward College are expected to engage in a significant research project, completed under the supervision of a faculty member. Some students propose projects that require a team approach with other students, but most engage in a research program on their own. Students may complete these projects during their junior or senior years, and must present their results and methodology to a seminar of students and faculty in the college.

The students in Ward are also expected to engage in ongoing service to their community or to others. Though this may occasionally result in an extended leave from the campus for some students, most often students remain involved in some form of service throughout their period of enrollment. Examples of service include volunteer work with older persons, recreational programs for disadvantaged youth, drug abuse programs, assistance at local schools in reading and math programs, work with retarded children, and clean-up projects for hospitals and other local institutions. While the Ward students are not required to serve in any one particular area, they are expected to develop a sense of service to others that is expressed in actual behavior.

Ward students are all engaged, at one time or another during their undergraduate years, in an international education program. For most of them this involves sutdying abroad for one of the summer terms, in Europe, Africa, or Asia. The international program is intended to give Ward students a new perspective on learning, on science, and on themselves. There is an extensive preparation program that lasts one year which students are required to take, and a specific individual project to complete while abroad. Once back on the home campus, students present their project to a faculty and student seminar. Although a substantive project is expected, there is considerable flexibility in terms of format, and previous student projects have included papers, debates, results of research, movies, and multimedia presentations.

The Ward College faculty have always made significant attempts to know their students, and to develop academic methods that would meet their needs. They have never been enthusiastic about educational fads, but neither are they close-minded about new approaches to learning. Students in the college enroll for at least one seminar per year, usually a group of no more than 12 students. Independent study is not only a possibility, but a requirement, as reflected by the research program. In the past three years, the faculty has been reasonably pleased with their experiments with a self-paced instructional program for some students in a biology course, and with the development of a "modular instructional package" in computer science. It is the college's intent to offer diverse learning opportunities and styles. The lecture is still used by many faculty, but there is a recognition that it is a method at which some faculty excel more than others.

Ward College enrolls a total of approximately 1,500 students, and usually about 200 of them will be abroad studying or engaged in an off-campus service project. The college is housed in a large multipurpose building which bears its name, and students reside in a series of six "houses" that encircle the academic building. Each of the houses has a faculty member who lives in the house, dining facilities, recreational space, and study areas. The houses are also equipped with computer terminals and closed-circuit television, for special individual work by students. Each house has its own identity and history, and vigorous forms of competition exist among them. The houses in Ward College are named after famous scientists. Currently the house names are Newton, Harvey, Curie, Einstein, Priestley, and Pasteur. Students are assigned to these houses at random during their first year, but after that time they may choose which one to live in, depending on available space. Although students are not required to live in the houses after their first two years, most elect to do so, because they constitute such an integral part of Ward College. Each of the Ward houses is represented on the Ward College Council, and each house carries on an extensive program of social, cultural, and recreational activities of its own. Much of the student leadership in the Ward houses has been traditionally supplied by juniors and seniors.

Although Ward is physically separate from the other two colleges, it is only about a five-minute walk to the residential and academic facilities of Jones and Morrison. The students interact frequently, as do the faculty, and as mentioned earlier, share the central Segar library, the Segar Community Center, and joint participation in the Assembly. In addition, they take at least one-quarter of their academic work in the other colleges.

The students come to Ward College primarily from within the state. Ward has established a reputation for excellence in science, and there are more applicants than can be admitted. About 10 percent of the college enrollment is from out of state, and there are 50 foreign students as well. Although previous academic performance weighs heavily in the admissions process, emphasis is also placed upon previous work in science and science-related fields. If an applicant can demonstrate her or his interest and aptitude for serious scientific work by the presentation of actual projects or ideas, it is quite likely she or he may be admitted. Although the college has had some fairly good success with an "early-admit" program for students with comparatively limited academic backgrounds and records, it is not yet pleased with the results. It remains committed to further attempts to encourage young people to enter scientific fields who have not been well represented in them previously. The "outreach" service work of many of the enrolled Ward students in secondary and elementary schools throughout the state is perhaps the most positive action being taken. Students in their early teens are quite likely to believe college-age persons when they show them what science can be, how mathematics is related to science, and how important science can be to the problems of people. The Ward students attempt to transmit some of their own enthusiasm to these young people in these service efforts.

There are many ways in which Ward College recognizes the work of its students. In addition to the usual academic honoraries (the college has the traditional grading system), outstanding work in academics, service work, athletics, research, and independent scientific writing are recognized each year in the college. The most prized recognition among students is to be voted a "John Ward scholar," an honor that is received by no more than fifteen seniors per year. These awardees exemplify the ideals of the college, and of Segar University, by their commitment to outstanding scholarship, service, and research.

Of growing concern in the past five years has been the large number of students in Ward who express a desire to attend medical and other professional schools, but who have difficulty getting accepted because of the large number of applicants nationwide. Although the faculty at Ward do not want to discourage student's aspirations, they are concerned that increasing numbers of students may be frustrated with their inability to get accepted to professional schools. The student's advising committee is of greatest help in this regard at Ward, but there are still problems. Students are not discouraged from changing their academic interests (or even their college at Segar), and attempts are made regularly to acquaint them with a wide-ranging knowlege about various careers. The record of Ward students being accepted to professional schools has been excellent over the years, but the current problem is that there are so many more students expressing professional school as their objective. In the fall of 1974, for example, 35 percent of the entering class at Ward said they wanted to become medical doctors. The college is presently working with the Advising Center staff in efforts to advise new applicants to the institution of this situation, and is assisting seniors explore other career alternatives in case they are not accepted to professional school.

Ward has cooperated for several years with the Office of Institutional

Studies at Segar in conducting research on its programs and graduates. Ward has reason to be pleased that the postcollege activities of its graduates seem to reflect in many ways the objectives of the college. A significant proportion of them have been active in their communities in service areas, many have continued their interests in international concerns, and many have made substantive intellectual contributions in various scientifically related disciplines. With the broad-based educational program at Ward, it is not surprising that many graduates are not directly involved in scientific professions, but are often in public life, industry, and government. Ward is currently emphasizing studies involving the postcollege activities of its women and minority graduates of the past ten years. Such information can prove helpful not only to current planning but also to future women and minority-group applicants.

Ward College tries to be not just a place for its students and faculty, but also a concept, or an ideal. It rarely talks about its own excellence, and tries not to compare itself with or model itself after some other institution. Above all, it hopes to create in its students a "sense of striving" for excellence. It is committed to the notion that science is exciting but hard work, and that it is necessarily related to people. It has not "found the final, correct way" for undergraduate education in the sciences, but is convinced that the continual and vigorous search for that ideal is the only appropriate business of its academic community.

Jones College. Jones College has existed since the founding of Segar University. It has its primary emphasis in the humanities and fine arts. It was named in 1947 after Aurora Jones, noted sculptor and a faculty member at Segar since its opening. Jones is a legendary figure at the college, and is regarded as an ideal "renaissance woman." She taught, spoke frequently around the country, was an accomplished violinist, a noted sculptor, and an indefatigable debater who spoke four languages. Her teaching inspired hundreds of undergraduates for years, and the energy she had for the university and its work seemed endless. When she "retired" in 1947, there was never any question that the college would be named in her honor. After several more years of creative work, she died in 1958 and left her estate to the college, the income from which now supports special international educational programs in fine arts.

Jones College strives to offer a high-quality liberal education with an emphasis upon the humanities and fine arts. It clearly has the strongest emphasis upon international education and cross-cultural studies of any of the three Segar colleges.

Jones College expects that all its students take basic courses in these core areas: foreign languages, history, literature and philosophy, fine arts (to include music, theater, art, and dance), and natural science. Students also engage in individual study in a field of concentration during their junior and senior years, enroll in at least one seminar per year, have an international experience, and participate in a service program. Finally, the students are able to elect at least one-third of their course work from the other colleges at Segar, with the approval of their advising committee.

Most of the Jones College students learn one foreign language very well, and many acquire a solid reading knowlege of at least one other. Most often, the language learned in depth is used in the country where the student engages in international study. In recent years, these countries have included Russia, India, Mexico, and several European and African countries. Although most frequently Jones students enroll in another university while studying abroad, it is also possible for them to engage in an independent project related to their area of concentration and interest. For example, one Jones student, whose field is photography, last winter traveled extensively through six African countries and took hundreds of pictures of young children in various kinds of school settings. His project will be a "traveling display" of these photographs to be used in American elementary schools located close to Segar. Another student pursued more traditional studies in philosophy and religion in England, and yet another spent her time in New Delhi, studying Indian music and its relationship to the Indian culture. Thus, the study of a foreign language has a directed purpose for students. Mastering it is necessary to achieve other important educational and personal goals. Many Jones students do not decide until their sophomore year what language to concentrate on, but most learn very rapidly, simply because of the need to learn. The college feels strongly that, for the international experience to be worthwhile, the students need a thorough orientation program before going, careful professional supervision while studying abroad, and personal follow-up and evaluation after returning to Jones. Although these commitments require time, money, and personnel, the college feels that they are essential to a successful international experience.

Jones students also are required to study history, literature, and philosophy, with the overall purpose being to gain more in-depth insights into the ideas, people, and customs of various cultures. The college believes that its students should have a broad liberal education that emphasizes Eastern and Western cultures, and should also study one particular culture in depth. From this concentrated study often students develop an interest in a particular aspect of that culture which becomes the subject of their senior thesis. For example, a student whose area of concentration was French literature studied French culture in depth for two years as part of his independent work, and later did his senior thesis on Stendahl. Many of the courses in these areas at Jones are taught by faculty from different disciplines, in an effort to emphasize the interrelationship of history, literature, and philosophy. Students are required to do a considerable amount of writing in these courses, usually of a critical nature concerning various ideas, concepts, and theories of life. They are then often called upon to defend their point of view of analysis in the lively and open discussions that are a "trademark" of Jones classes.

Jones students also take a considerable amount of work in music, theater, art, and dance. While not all Jones students, of course, enter the fields these areas represent, the college feels strongly that students benefit not only from a knowledge of these fine arts, but also from actual experiences within them. The program for students in this core area attempts to combine breadth and depth, the intellectual and the experiential. Thus students study the music, theater, art, and dance of several cultures, again with an emphasis upon their relationship to the values and customs of those cultures. They also are asked to concentrate their study for a period of time in a specific area, such as dance, and to become personally involved in one of the numerous Jones College or community fine arts groups. For example, a Jones student may study generally in the fine arts for all four years, but during this time, the student might become especially knowledgeable about the music of African countries, and, with other members of the college or community, form a small musical group that learns how to play (hopefully to a tolerable level of skill) these new musical instruments. In the Jones College community, finding other such interested individuals is never difficult, and a willing (if not always enthusiastic!) audience can usually be arranged.

Jones students are required to have a basic general education in the natural sciences, which is intended to acquaint students with science as a method of inquiry as well as an additional tool to use in the understanding of a culture. For this part of the academic core, Jones students mix freely in classes with Ward College, especially during the first and second years. As with the Ward program, the emphasis is upon the relationship of science to humans and the effect science has upon culture, ideas, and people.

Besides the strong emphasis upon international study and independent work, Jones students are expected to engage in service programs while undergraduates. At Jones, where there is so much diversity among the students and their interests, these service programs have been extensive. A few examples will illustrate. John, an especially talented dancer and a senior, has for two years worked as a volunteer in a county school system, half a day per week helping to instruct elementary school children in dance; Joyce, a sophomore with an interest in painting as therapy for the mentally ill, has volunteered her services at a state hospital in an informal, experimental instructional program; Willis, a senior in theater arts, has assisted the local high school drama department in teaching students how to build stage scenery, backdrops, and equipment; and Theresa, a junior in music, has cooperated with a program in a neighboring community whose purpose it is to acquaint disadvantaged children with various kinds of music, and to encourage them to learn how to play a musical instrument. The tradition for this kind of service at Jones is sufficiently strong that the students usually seek out or create most of these involvements on their own. The student's advising committee must hear the proposal for the project and approve it. The project must, in some way, be related to the student's major course of study, and the student must be prepared to evaluate her or his service experiences to that same critical advising committee. Service is not viewed as a burden by the students or the college, but as a "real-life" experience, in the field that gives the student a chance to test his or her abilities and ideas. It is also consistent, of course, with the educational outcomes the college wants to encourage among its students.

A unique experience is available to Jones students who elect to "participate." It is called the "Free Semester" program. Recognizing that many students get so caught up in the relatively structured "grind" of going to school year after year that they may never get a chance to "take a good look at themselves," the faculty decided in 1964 to experiment with the "free semester." Students who "participate" are not required to engage in any form of formal study, either in class or independently. They do not have to complete any assignments, and do not even have to stay in the local community. Although any student may, of course, drop out of school any semester, this free semester program is intended as a conscious, rational effort to provide the student with a period of self-reflection. Although only about a third of Jones students participate in this program, their experiences with it and reactions to it have been sufficiently positive to convince the faculty to continue it.

Another program that is a tradition at Jones College is the Undergraduate Fellowship program, begun in the 1950s to encourage students to consider college teaching as a career. Although the need in 1975 is not as great for college teachers, the program is still very popular, as there are a number of students in the college who intend to become college teachers. A form of internship, the program affords students an opportunity to work closely with an assigned faculty tutor, and to become personally acquainted with the field of college teaching through him or her. The student may become familiar with the day-to-day problems of faculty both in and out of the classroom, and may be given supervised opportunities to teach first-year classes for brief periods. Students apply and are selected for these "fellowships," which include no financial remuneration but are considered to be a valuable opportunity for junior and senior students.

Students at Jones are encouraged to participate in special educational and developmental workshops offered both on and off campus. The faculty recognizes that such experiences can help clarify issues for students and assist them in learning more about themselves and their abilities. In addition to the large number of workshops in the various areas of music, art, drama, and dance, students have also participated in value-clarification workshops, leadership symposia, premarriage seminars, career planning workshops, and international perspectives workshops. The students' advising committees approve these experiences for the Jones undergraduates, and while they are not overtly negative to the "search for one's identity" type of experience, they are cautious of educational fads, and have emphasized more substantive experiences in past years for their student advisees.

Jones College, like Ward and Morrison, is a place. It comprises five separate but related buildings, two of which are entirely instructional in nature, the other three of which combine instructional, performance, and residential space. Students reside in Haydn, Joyce, and Monet Halls, names decided upon some years ago by the Jones Town Council. The College Hall is the main building that houses classrooms and faculty offices, and the Fine Arts Lab is the home for a small experimental theater, dance space, sculpture rooms, music practice rooms, and painting areas. Although most of the students live in the residential areas, they are not required to do so. Also included in the three residential buildings are additional small fine arts space, recreational and social space, facilities for computer-related instruction, and a few faculty offices. The Jones College area is located within a few hundred yards of all other facilities on the campus, including the other colleges.

Although the description of Jones College thus far has emphasized the curricular and relatively formal aspects of its program, the college is perhaps best known for its informal yet highly stimulating "extracurricular life." If anything is sacred at Jones College, it is the "absolute relativeness" of everything—ideas, programs, and procedures! No one would ever dare claim that something was not subject to debate or question; in fact, nothing in Jones College seems ever to go undebated. The students quickly become acquainted with this atmosphere, although there are quite a few egos that need rebuilding after first being confronted in class, over a cup of coffee, after a game of soccer, or during a Jones Town Council meeting by an older student or faculty member. No one, however, attacks people at Jones—just their ideas, and the assumptions upon which they are based. There is a very strong conviction in the Jones community that learning takes place best in settings where people know each other and are not hesitant to test out their ideas on others, even though they may be "embarrassed" in the process. Although this conviction is well known to all, it, like the overall excellence of the college, is rarely verbalized. It is not surprising that the Jones College debate team has consistently placed among the nation's best in competition; however, team members themselves admit there is more fun and challenge to a Jones Town Council meeting than to most intercollegiate debating matches.

Although the college strongly emphasizes public speaking in its curriculum, students seem to develop these skills very adequately almost in self-defense, or in spite of the college's formal efforts! There are many student-faculty dramatic productions throughout the year, both traditional and innovative, and many are written by students and faculty of the college. There are several Jones dance groups, four jazz bands, a Jones College symphony, the Jones College artists' guild, arts and crafts groups, rock groups, string quartets, madrigal singers, glee clubs, and numerous other activities. Virtually all students and faculty of the college participate in some group. For several years, student musical, artistic, and dance groups have traveled widely in the United States, and several have traveled abroad as well. Some faculty claim that Jones is "more than just a college—it is an authentic laboratory for the arts—with a distinctive personality." Although the competitiveness of the student body is evident, there are a friendliness and a great respect for diversity as well. Although student members of Segar's other colleges delight in teasing Jones students about the "organizational chaos" they perceive at Jones (as epitomized by the Jones Town Council), the Jones students proudly respond, with tongue in cheek, that "that is how truly creative people operate." Another important part of the Jones tradition is the well-known but rarely verbalized notion that "agreement is not necessary, and perhaps not desirable." Jones students learn that friendships and effective work can proceed while not everyone in is in agreement on all issues; moreover, they seem to grow from the diversity that exists, and love to poke fun at those who assume that the aim of "communication" is to resolve all differences.

The college has struggled hard in recent years not to become an elitist or "honors" institution. It is well aware that much of its program, both formal and informal, might seem worthwhile only to the daughters and sons of college-educated people. It has made a conscious effort in the last ten years to recruit a student body as diverse in background as the college is in its emphasis. It has had considerable success with these efforts, but realizes that much of its good fortune is tied to its excellent reputation and its good record of assisting its graduates in getting jobs and in being accepted to professional schools. The current economic situation is presenting some of the most severe tests to Jones and its traditions, and the next five to ten years will prove to be very crucial to the college's future.

Morrison College. Morrison College was founded in 1941, and was named after Carl Morrison, one of the original faculty members at Segar University. Dr. Morrison was a national recognized political scientist, and a State

Department official during the 1930s. He chaired the committee that created the college, and remained on the Segar faculty until his retirement in 1946. The overall emphasis of Morrison College is in the social and behavioral sciences. The college strives, through its curricular and out-of-class programs, to create in its students a "world view" of social and political problems. It assumes that most of its graduates will enter fields of public service, government, teaching, and law. Since the college began, more than half of Morrison's students have gone on to graduate school in the various social and behavioral sciences, education, and law.

Students in Morrison College are required to take a core of courses in each of the following areas: history and government; political science and philosophy; psychology and sociology; economics; and natural sciences. A number of Morrison students enter the teaching field directly upon receiving the bachelor's degree, and these students also take courses that assist them in their teaching responsibilities.

While there is this required core of courses in specific areas at Morrison, there is considerable flexibility in the curriculum. Students take almost half their courses as electives, many of which are in the other two colleges at Segar University. Morrison College emphasizes off-campus learning experiences and internships more than any other college at Segar. In accordance with their advising committee, students participate in both service programs and off-campus internships, for credit, which are related to their academic interests and personal commitments. Morrison students are regularly involved in local, state, national, and international governmental internships. For example, one student spent a year as a participant-observer on a task force appointed by the city commission to reorganize municipal government. Another student worked as a legislative intern at the state capital, where the assignment with an individual legislator was to research other states' legislative programs in the area of social services. Finally, another student spent two summers with a regional office of the Department of Health, Education, and Welfare, learning about the development and implementation of educational programs for preschool children.

As indicated earlier, Morrison College has always had a strong commitment to helping students obtain a "world view" of social problems and issues. Morrison makes significant efforts to bring international political and intellectual leaders to the college for short periods of time to provide additional perspectives on social issues and problems. Approximately 15 percent of the student body at Morrison comes from other countries, and these students serve as a valuable learning resource for the college as well. All the Morrison students spend at least one term in another country while they are undergraduates, and this is arranged and approved by the student's academic advising committee. The student is given a specific project to complete in accordance with his or her study in a foreign country. While many of these foreign study projects have concerned analyses of governmental operations in various countries, Morrison students have also studied hospitals, schools, prison systems, and social services in other countries. The college's strong interest in encouraging careers in public administration is enhanced by this program for its students, and the college believes that with continued close supervision, the foreign-study projects will continue to be a significant part of the undergraduate educational program.

The college also believes that students need real-life experiences if they are going to become effective public administrators and leaders of social change in the society. As one effort in this area, the college has initiated a series of programs called "urban plunges," during which time small groups of students and faculty visit an American city for a short period of time—usually about two weeks. During this "plunge" period, the students and the faculty investigate on an intensive basis some predetermined problems in that city. They become involved with the people concerned with those problems, discuss them in great detail, and then together arrive at various "solutions" to these problems. The "urban plunge" program has proved to be greatly successful and popular among both students and faculty.

Morrison has also had good success with the "flip side" of the urban plunge program in which various community leaders from a town or city in the state are invited to the college for an intensive three-day experience with students and faculty. During this time, the community leaders not only are introduced to the campus and the college, but also engage in all-day seminars on the problems they are facing in their community. Thus, the "university plunge" becomes an excellent laboratory on the campus for the Morrison students as well as an effective learning experience for the community leaders.

Although the academic terms at Morrison coincide with those of Ward and Jones, the comparatively large number of internships and off-campus experiences for the Morrison students have resulted in the increased use of "learning contracts" between students and faculty members. Most students and faculty have been pleased with these contracts, and as long as a student can convince his or her academic advising committee of the value of a proposed program, the student can proceed.

Morrison's governance structure consists of a house and a senate, both composed of faculty members and students, elected at large by members of the college itself. There is a Morrison College constitution, which serves as the basis of the governance process. The dean of Morrison chairs the "joint session" when it meets, but the house and senate of Morrison elect their own leaders each year. In some cases it has been a student, but most often it is a faculty member. Perhaps reflecting the curriculum and the overall purposes of the college, the house and the senate at Morrison are generally more formal and more oriented to "due-process-type procedures" than the governance bodies of the other two colleges or of Segar University as a whole. There is a strong commitment to rather predictable procedures, and also to democratic decisionmaking. Although there are vigorous debates, many questions are settled on the basis of the Morrison constitution and the various rules and regulations that have been developed over the years.

Although a high percentage of the Morrison graduates in recent years have gone on to professional and graduate schools, Morrison is not an honors college, and has actively recruited students from broad social and economic backgrounds in order to maintain balance in its student body. Many of its graduates are now in college teaching positions, several work for the federal and state governments, and others are practicing attorneys. Morrison is especially proud of its record of having ten Rhodes Scholars in its relatively short history.

As with Ward and Jones, Morrison College is a place. The college itself is housed in a large building which includes classrooms, faculty offices, seminar rooms, auditoria, a small library, and reading rooms. Surrounding the main building for the college are the twelve Morrison houses, where the students reside. These houses, named by the Morrison house and senate for outstanding persons in public and academic life, are Parsons, Jefferson, Kennedy, Jung, Holmes, Darrow, Watson, Dix, Smith, James, Merton, and Brandeis. First- and second-year students are required to live in these houses, but juniors and seniors continue to live on campus for the educational and social benefits that living in these houses provides them. Each house is assigned a faculty tutor, who has an apartment in the house, but who does not reside permanently there. The houses have developed personalities of their own over the years, and there is lively competition among them, both in academics and in extracurricular activities.

There are a large number of student organizations associated with Morrison College in areas as diverse as sports, recreation, politics, international affairs, social activites, and religious concerns. A source of particular pride over the years in Morrison College has been the large number of publications that have emerged from the college, most of them results of student initiative. The *Morrison Review*, a quarterly commentary on political and social events, with articles written by students, is the best known of these. Frequently included in this publication are articles adapted from the foreign service projects engaged in by Morrison students. There are several forms of recognition that students may receive in Morrison, but the most prized is the "Carl Morrison Fellow" designation. Approximately five juniors and ten seniors each year are so designated by the faculty of the college for their outstanding achievement in academic work, service projects, and commitment to international relations.

Morrison College strives to develop an atmosphere in which students might pursue the social and behavioral sciences in a way that will help them develop a world view of social and economic problems. There is strong emphasis upon the development of leadership in its students, and the college strives to help students learn how to be effective participants and agents of change in the social process. Not surprisingly, during the 1960s, there was a great deal of turmoil in Morrison College, especially as it related to the activities of this country in the Indo-China war, and the social policies of the U.S. government. While this was a difficult period for the college, strenuous efforts were made to get students involved in those issues and problems as learning situations that might contribute to students' academic and professional goals.

The Student Advising Program

As mentioned earlier, Segar University feels strongly that if it is to have a significant impact upon its students, it has to get to know them as persons, and to establish close relationships between faculty and students. It is this concern that has led the university to its strong commitment to its student advising program. Upon entrance to the university, a student is assigned a faculty advisor, who chairs the academic advising committee for the student. The committee also includes a member of the Student Advising Center and another faculty member in the university. This group of three staff members stays with the same student for the entire period of four years as the advising committee, and has a considerable amount of authority regarding that student's academic program. The committee is authorized to approve a program of study within the colleges' guidelines, and to arrange appropriate international service programs and projects for the student. The academic advising program is a costly one for Segar University, because it entails a great deal of faculty time and commitment. However, no other program in the university is more important to the attainment of the desired student outcomes than this one. Besides the time involved in getting an academic course of study approved, each student spends a required eight hours during the period of four years in attendance at Segar with his/her academic advising committee, and among many other things, discusses at least the following in these interview situations: personal background of the student—family, school, previous experiences, reasons for coming to Segar; personal values, goals, and aspirations; academic interests and abilities; summer experiences while in college; cocurricular and informal involvement at Segar; international education and service project participation; reassessment of personal values, goals, and aspirations; and final consideration of years spent at Segar.

Although this program takes a good deal of time, because it is individualized, virtually all students and faculty at Segar University are convinced of its value. Although sometimes the academic advising committee serves as a "prodder" to students and requires more things of the student than he or she would like, for most students the academic advising committee constitutes a highly significant experience. Many Segar graduates maintain contact with their advising committee members long after they leave Segar. This effort is a recognition that the development of students and the impact of Segar as a whole are the result of a great variety of experiences for students—not just those in the classroom. It is also a recognition on the part of the Segar faculty that academic advising is an extremely important activity for undergraduates that can have a significant impact upon their choice of careers and professional aspirations.

Other University Services

Although the colleges are very autonomous, there are some universitywide services. Of particular note is the Office of the Coordinator of International and Service Studies. This office provides assistance to the colleges, makes arrangements for the many details that are involved in these programs, and offers expertise and experience in the handling of them. The Office of Institutional Studies cooperates with the colleges and the university president in conducting studies on Segar students and especially the impact that the college has upon their plans, attitudes, and aspirations. The Segar University Library is centralized and serves as the primary resource facility for each of the colleges. The Office of the Coordinator of Student Advising programs also serves in a coordinating role for student financial aid programs, placement, and new student orientation to Segar.

Although much of the life of Segar is centered in the colleges and in the residential houses making up each of the colleges, a considerable amount of universitywide activity for students also takes place. Besides the formal activity at the Segar University Assembly, there are a number of athletic teams at both the intercollegiate and the intramural levels. Although each of the colleges has its own commencement ceremonies, the tradition is that everyone participates in a total Segar commencement as well. There is a good deal of humorous and good-natured competition among the colleges at virtually every universitywide event, but the all-university graduation ceremony seems to epitomize this competition. Students and faculty take great pride in their colleges, and there seems to be no end to the creative ways in which this is expressed, especially in public ceremonies.

Segar University does not claim to be especially innovative in either its particular educational programs or its governance structure. Rather, it has attempted to define its mission within the scope and ability of its facilities and faculty. It is strongly committed to undergraduate education, and has resisted efforts to expand the college in ways that are not in accordance with its basic educational objective. Although not negative to graduate education, it continues to feel that the existence of major graduate programs on campus may have a detrimental effect upon its commitment to undergraduate education. It believes that its academic programs will be effective in direct relationship to the clarity of its objectives, the personal nature of its program, and the quality of its teaching. It is strongly committed to its six stated educational goals for students: (1) intellectual competence; (2) international understanding; (3) service to society; (4) a sense of values; (5) a sense of personal confidence; and (6) facility of expression. It attempts to know its students both statistically and personally, and makes conscious efforts to recruit students in accordance with its educational philosophy. While it recognizes that it does not and cannot serve all the needs of all the students who are seeking higher education, it is attempting to fulfill its particular role with groups of students who are attracted to its various programs. Segar is continuously striving for excellence and for new ways in which to develop effective educational programs. It does not apologize for its efforts to learn from other institutions and to adapt its programs where it has found that they are lacking. Segar was founded less than forty years ago as an effort to develop undergraduate education in a way that can affect the lives and future directions of students. It remains committed to this goal as its primary mission.

References

Bell, Daniel. *The Reforming of General Education*. New York: Anchor Books. 1966.

Change Magazine. *The Yellow Pages of Undergraduate Innovations*. Cornell Center for Improvement in Undergraduate Education. 1974.

Gaff, Jerry G., and Associates. *The Cluster College*. San Francisco: Jossey-Bass. 1970.

Levine, Arthur, and Weingart, John. *Reform of Undergraduate Education*. San Francisco: Jossey-Bass. 1973.

Martin, W.B. *Alternative to Irrelevance*. Nashville, Tenn.: Abingdon. 1968.

6

Undergraduate Education: Recommendations for Action

In the first five chapters of this book, various problems in undergraduate education were described, the changing nature of the student population was noted, the research on impact of institutions was reviewed, and a case description of a hypothetical institution was presented. The case was made for greater commitment to undergraduate education and for educational programs that can influence the lives of students. It is the thesis of this book that there is a crisis in undergraduate education; that there is an urgent need to institute reforms in many college and university programs. Even with the very difficult problems currently being faced by most institutions of higher education, there seems to be a favorable climate for this reform. Many colleges and universities have initiated changes in various areas, but too often these have occurred in relatively isolated places, and only small "pockets" of the campus have been affected. These changes usually represent the activities of only a few professors or administrators, not the institution as a whole.

It has also been emphasized that undergraduate programs should be developed on the basis of the institutions' desired outcomes for students. Often programs have been planned and maintained without adequate regard for their impact on students. Insufficient evaluation of undergraduate programs has also existed, despite the excellent instruments now available for this purpose. The increasing diversity in the undergraduate student population has not yet stimulated enough institutions to make adjustments in their academic and student service programs to meet the needs of these "new" students.

The hypothetical institutional model presented in Chapter 5 was not intended to be "the answer" to all the problems in undergraduate education. Rather, this case description of "Segar University" was designed to illustrate how one institution might organize its learning environments and develop educational programs for undergraduates in ways that reflect a specific set of objectives. It was presented as one model among many needed ones to address the wide diversity of students and curricula. Finally, it attempted to demonstrate that one institution cannot be "all things to all people," but must decide on its own role and develop programs in accordance with that role.

The purpose of this final chapter is to suggest specific actions that institutions might consider in efforts to make their undergraduate programs more effective for students. It is recognized that some of these recommendations may not fit the needs of each individual institution. The recommendations assume, of course, that there is a generally shared desire among leaders in higher education to improve the quality of undergraduate education.

Goals and Purposes

Institutions should develop an educational philosophy and strive to make it known and understood by their students, faculty, alumni, and friends.

No other recommendation in this chapter is more important than this one. An institution needs not only to know itself, but to have its mission well understood by the people it serves. There are important differences among colleges and universities, and the distinctive educational character of each needs to be described in detail. Students can benefit greatly by knowing and understanding what an institution's actual educational purposes are—when they apply for admission, as they matriculate, and in their role as alumni. This educational philosophy should not be so broad and vague so as to include everything in all higher education. The current lack of coherence in so many undergraduate programs is, in many ways, a reflection of the absence of any distinctive educational philosophy. The stated purpose of the college's educational program must be consistent with its role and ability to deliver that program. Each institution cannot be excellent in every academic area of higher education—but each institution can work toward developing a distinctive character of its own. This process is difficult for many colleges and universities, of course, since so many of them cannot resist growth, money, or other opportunities for expansion. If they are really committed to building an undergraduate program that represents a coherent educational purpose, they will expand only in ways that are consistent with that purpose.

Educational objectives should be developed in relationship to desired student outcomes, and should be regularly evaluated by the institution.

Although there is no implication here that colleges and universities should strive to get students to fit into some predetermined mold, the institution should have a clear idea of the educational outcomes it is working for in its students. These "outcomes" are often so vague and broad that they are meaningless. An institution can and should define specific and measurable impacts it desires to have upon its students, such as levels of intellectual competence, facility of expression, or a sense of service to others. When a college defines its objectives in such terms, both students and faculty can benefit, as there is some overall direction for their activities. Too much of undergraduate education is not connected well to the lives of undergraduates, and too many academic programs are planned and maintained that do not reflect any real outcomes for these students. Regular evaluation of the effectiveness of the educational program in meeting these desired student outcomes can contribute greatly to better understanding, and is necessary for planning and revision of programs. Educational goals should reflect the desired educational outcomes for undergraduates, and should not simply be "tucked away in the catalog" and forgotten.

Organization and Administration

The organizational structure of institutions should reflect a commitment to a coherent program of undergraduate education.

Many institutions could benefit from a careful reassessment of their organizational structure. Often this structure is a reflection of historical accident, a desire for expansion, or simply rampant departmentalism more than the result of a conscious effort to present a unified and sensible undergraduate program. Specific subunits of the institution, especially those with good funding, may be very separate from other academic areas. The only relationship an undergraduate student may perceive between departments or colleges is an incidental one. Although such isolated arrangements may be viewed as productive and desirable by some faculty, there must be efforts made to extend the concerns of faculty to campuswide academic issues. Current organizational structures are a function more of the professional preferences of the faculty than of the educational needs of the undergraduates. Efforts to reorganize educational structures, of course, are fraught with difficulties, as they represent real threats to academic and personal empires on the campus and are likely to meet vigorous resistance. The fragmented nature of much of undergraduate education today is largely the result of these competing and often noncommunicating academic "fiefdoms" on a campus. Cooperation with other organizational units on campus is sometimes pursued only with caution, as a department may not want to relinquish its competitive position or prestige. Effecting change in such situations will require courageous and imaginative leadership from administrators. However, administration has become so involved in issues not directly related to the academic program itself that its impact upon internal educational matters has often been minimal.

In the large universities with extensive graduate programs, the need for a careful organizational reassessment of undergraduate education is most crucial. Where there are extensive graduate programs, there is almost always a diminishing of the role of undergraduate education. There are exceptions, of course, and in many such cases there is an organizational structure at the complex university that is devoted to undergraduate education. Such arrangements are necessary in order to demonstrate the commitment of the institution to undergraduate studies, and to make more possible the integration of the curriculum. A dean or a provost for undergraduate education, provided with adequate authority and responsibility, can have a very positive influence on a large campus. Although the organizational structure is an important indication of the institution's commitment to undergraduate education, it cannot bring about change itself. Presidents must exert leadership in the educational program, and must become more involved in undergraduate education. Without such leadership, individual "pockets" of the campus will continue to "do their own thing," apart from any coherent and organized approach to undergraduate learning.

Institutions should organize their academic structures to account for the impact of size.

During the past fifteen years, when enrollments grew at such a rapid rate, too many institutions simply added large numbers of students and faculty, but retained essentially the same administrative structure. In many cases an impersonal and ineffective education for undergraduates resulted. Students had very large classes, especially as first- and second-year students, and few received personalized academic advising. While an administrative structure might be adequate for 5,000 students, it probably would not be for 20,000 students. Institutions should review their academic organizational arrangements in light of their goals for undergraduate education as they relate to the problem of size. Large size can be handled well and can be an educational asset, but the institution must organize for it. The creation of semiautonomous "clusters" on a large campus is one effective way not only to combat the problems of size, but also to create smaller, more personalized academic units that can have an identity for students. As was indicated in the review of research on impact in Chapter 4, size can be a negative influence upon undergraduates unless the institution organizes its program in personal ways for the student.

Institutions should work to create a greater sense of community among students, faculty, and administration.

There is no implication here that "agreement" is needed among various groups on a campus. Rather, it is being argued that colleges and universities are unique organizations, and should exert special efforts to bring students, faculty, and administrators closer together regarding the affairs of the institution. Although formal representation on committees is important in this regard, more crucial is the day-by-day interaction among these groups. Campuses that can create and maintain this "spirit" have lower dropout rates, better morale, and more positive impact upon their students, again as indicated in Chapter 4.

Although an organizational structure can contribute to this sense of community on a campus, the attitudes that faculty and administrators demonstrate with students are more important. Where students feel genuine concern from faculty and administration for their educational and personal growth, a sense of community is much more likely to exist. In many of our larger and commuter-oriented campuses, the amount of contact students have with faculty is quite small, and it is more difficult to create this sense of community. Special efforts should be made by these institutions to meet this need for undergraduates. The "layers of bureaucracy" that some institutions have created between students and "the university" have contributed to feelings of alienation and work at cross purposes with a feeling of community. To some undergraduates, the university may be viewed as no different than a large corporation, with hundreds of "employees" that all have their own little set of concerns, with no one being able (or willing) to speak for the whole. Such perceptions may have a detrimental effect upon the quality of undergraduate education, and they are difficult to change. However, if the institution is serious about its undergraduate program and wants to create a better sense of community on campus, it can make significant improvements by decreasing the layers of bureaucracy and by demonstrating more positive attitudes and humane concern for its undergraduates.

Academic Programs

Institutions should re-commit themselves to the importance of undergraduate teaching.

The quality of teaching at an institution is its most important characteristic. In many institutions, especially larger ones with extensive graduate programs, undergraduate teaching has become a low priority and has not been recognized or rewarded adequately by the institution. The teaching of undergraduates, especially at the first- and second-year levels, has frequently been viewed as a burden or as an assignment to be given to faculty members with the least amount of seniority or prestige. At some of the larger universities, over half the teaching at the first- and second-year levels is done by teaching assistants who are graduate students. While many of these persons do an excellent job and are dedicated to their task, it is unlikely that they are as effective as experienced professors. It is not being argued that all institutions should completely reorder their established priorities in teaching assignments. However, it is strongly suggested that teaching assignments be reassessed and greater attention given to having experienced professors teach undergraduates on a regular basis, especially in the first and second years. Such a commitment by an institution to the value of undergraduate teaching can have a very positive influence on students early in their college careers. It also can serve to counteract the current impression of many undergraduates that they are unimportant or unworthy of the attention of the "real professors." Institutions will succeed in these efforts to the extent that they provide adequate rewards and recognition to faculty members for such activities. Many faculty will respond positively to a diversity of teaching experiences, rather than having the same schedule year after year. The value of undergraduate teaching needs to be reemphasized, and colleges and universities can do a great deal by recognizing and rewarding excellence in teaching. Until such commitments are made, other efforts by the institution to improve its undergraduate educational program will be largely ineffectual.

Colleges and universities should strive to decrease the fragmentation of knowledge in the undergraduate curriculum and work to integrate it into an organized program for undergraduates.

An examination of student transcripts at many institutions today would reveal an almost incredible amount of confusion in undergraduate educational "programs." Many of these transcripts include lists of courses that are largely unrelated and do not reflect any overall plan, on the part of either the student or the institution. At some institutions, as long as a minimal number of "requirements" have been met, virtually any list of courses will qualify a student for a degree, provided that the credit total meets the requirements of the computer. While it is not being argued that there is a need for uniformity in the curriculum for all students, it is suggested that students and institutions need to develop a sense of coherence in their undergraduate programs. With the rampant departmentalism that exists on many campuses, students often graduate with the impression that knowledge is not interrelated, and they may have had very little experience outside of their own discipline. Consequently the connection between academic work and life is often seen as fleeting or nonexistant. Colleges and universities should strive in their undergraduate curricula to integrate the sciences with the humanities, the theoretical with the practical, and learning with living. The isolation of academic departments, though seen as valuable by some faculty, needs to be discontinued, so that undergraduate education can become truly interdisciplinary. The separation that exists between the curriculum and the "extracurriculum" represents a false dichotomy, and one that makes little sense in the lives of students. To address these difficult but important problems, colleges and universities must make major efforts to an institutionwide nature. The easier and more typical approach of minor policy changes or piecemeal "reforms" will not suffice. Presidentially appointed task forces or "commissions on undergraduate education'' should be formed and should be given specific assignments. With vigorous leadership from the president and other academic administrators, the needed integration of under-graduate education can be achieved on many campuses.

Institutions should recommit themselves to the value of general education.

Although the experience with programs in general education since the end of World War II has been uneven, the various shortcomings in these programs should not cause institutions to drop their commitment to the value of general education altogether. Effective programs in general education should be made part of the total curriculum, and should not be separate academic units. A general education core offered over a period of four years can increase undergraduate understanding of various cultures, social issues, and scientific problems. Often students do not have the benefit of such broad educational exposure except through general education. When general education courses are only offered at the first- and second-year levels, it is difficult for students to relate this knowlege to their total academic interests and goals. However, if there is flexibility in the program, so that students have a range of choices during their total period of enrollment, and if faculty are rewarded for supporting it, general education can succeed. In order to understand the complex problems of society, students must have educational experiences that go beyond the interests of specialized academic departments. The values of general education are too important to discard, and should become part of the total undergraduate program.

Colleges and universities should take advantage of the current positive climate for reform in undergraduate education.

Many innovations have been introduced in undergraduate education recently, and the climate for change is generally favorable, despite (or perhaps because of) rather gloomy economic conditions and the difficulty in attracting students to some institutions. However, much of this innovation and reform is hardly noticed, and does not represent a campuswide effort at change. While there may be small "pockets" of the campus that are actively engaged in new approaches to undergraduate education, most often these are not reflected in the academic programs for the majority of the undergraduates on the campus. Reform and innovation need to take into account the presence of the "new" students in higher education and the diverse learning styles that they represent. More frequent opportunities should be provided for students to explore various careers while engaged in academic work and independent study, and off-campus learning experiences should be expanded. Many institutions have gained favorable results in the past few years with such techniques as self-paced and modular instruction and computer-assisted teaching. These programs can be expanded to include more students and academic areas. Centers for educational innovation should be established on campuses, and information should be shared among institutions. While there have been some educational gimmicks and fads which should be rejected, the willingness to experiment with new educational techniques should be supported by presidents and other academic administrators.

Colleges and universities should give more attention to the evaluation of their students.

There has been a good deal of national attention given recently to the "inflated grades" that students are receiving at many undergraduate institutions. The increasing competition among students for admission to graduate and professional schools has been suggested as one cause for this grade inflation, as has the "nonpunitive" grading philosophy that has emerged in recent years. While the particular method of academic evaluation should be left up to each institution, a form of effective feedback to students about the quality of their academic work is essential to the learning process. In many instances now, undergraduates view the grading system as a sham, especially when all students in some courses receive A's and B's. What is needed is a more personalized and individualized academic evaluation. Even though it is costly and time-consuming, faculty should be expected to spend time with their students in personally assessing the quality of their work. Students are "called to task" all too infrequently during their undergraduate careers to defend or to justify a particular point of view presented in a paper, an idea or project presented at a seminar, or a creative piece of work they have done over a period of time. The emphasis upon grades as the means to a job or professional school must be lessened, for it obscures the real educational purposes of the academic evaluation of students. Though many undergraduates are "hell-bent" on getting a grade, they often become even more cynical about the process when they spend a great deal of time on a project, turn it in to a faculty member, and get back nothing more than a grade for the project. Students have a need for critical feedback and discussion of their educational work with faculty in order to learn from their mistakes, their shortcomings, and their misperceptions. Greater attention and more time must be given to the academic evaluation of undergraduates.

Colleges and universities should improve academic advising for undergraduate students.

On many campuses, especially large universities with graduate programs, the most frequently heard student complaint has to do with inadequate or unconcerned academic advising. Academic advising is often viewed as a low-level activity by faculty members, and on large campuses it is virtually impossible for individual faculty to know all the requirements in each academic major. Academic advising is usually not given much recognition in the evaluation process for faculty, and is viewed as a burden for them. It is also often viewed merely as a mechanical process, having to do with registration and "fulfilling the requirements." Students rapidly get caught up in this depersonalized situation, and learn to manipulate the system for their own ends. They may become highly cynical about their academic program, and see no real relationship between their academic work and their planned career. Academic advising is usually too separate from career counseling and has not approached the student in any holistic way. Many students have drifted from one major to another, often aimlessly, and without any overall direction or feedback from faculty. While it is not being argued that faculty should determine the academic majors for students or the particular course that their lives should follow, institutions should take a much more aggressive and positive role in academic advising programs. They should recognize that individual faculty members cannot know all the requirements in a large catalog, and should organize academic advising centers, staffed by professionals who can work with students and faculty members to serve students most effectively. Faculty cannot and should not be divorced from the process, but must remain involved with students and their academic and professional aspirations. The relationship that can develop between a student and a faculty member as a result of effective academic advising can comprise the most influential impact upon a student during his or her undergraduate career. However, personal and regular attention to the needs of these students is essential. Colleges and universities should address themselves to this problem, and recognize it as a crucial one in their undergraduate program.

Institutions should commit themselves to the value of international education for undergraduates.

Colleges and universities should recognize that most of their undergraduates have limited views of the world, which are conditioned by their lack of familiarity with different cultures and different peoples. Students can gain a great deal from international educational experiences, and can learn to understand more about themselves and the origin of their own cultures and ideas by significant involvement in other cultures. The world is increasingly interdependent; with modern communications, it is necessary for students to be aware of various problems in other countries and knowledgeable about their history, development, and people. Not all undergraduates have to "study abroad" in order to gain such understanding. Virtually every faculty has international expertise and experience included in it, and most colleges also have substantial numbers of international students. These resources can be used in academic and cocurricular programs on the campus. The traditionally heavy emphasis in general education on Western cultures should be expanded to include more about the cultures of other areas of the world. If institutions feel it important to help students overcome their provincialism and develop a "world view" toward learning, then a strong emphasis upon international education will be evident in their undergraduate program.

Institutional Research

Colleges and universities should establish offices of institutional research.
Too often institutions study almost everything but themselves and their own programs. An office of institutional research, given adequate funding and recognition, and reporting to the chief executive officer of the institution, can serve a very positive function on the campus. Such an office can provide excellent information that can be of great importance in decision-making and educational planning. It can help the institution focus upon campuswide problems and to understand better the nature of its organization. It can assist in establishing a well-organized data collection system that provides base-line information for the institution in its decisionmaking. Frequently decisions are made and plans established for institutions without enough information being gathered or evaluation having taken place. There are many excellent research instruments available for these purposes, and the status of institutional research has grown significantly over the past few years. The research office should be directly responsible to the president of the institution so that it can exercise maximum independence in its selection of research and evaluation projects for the benefit of the institution. Specific academic and student services programs should also be evaluated in relationship to the objectives established for them. In student services, for example, it is too often assumed that students are being well served by such programs as career counseling and placement, or financial aid, although there may have never been any systematic evaluation of them done. A thoughtful program of institutional research is really essential to the development of an effective program of undergraduate education.

Colleges and universities should study their impacts as institutions upon their students.
As argued previously, institutions should formulate specific objectives for their educational programs for undergraduates, in terms that can be evaluated. This emphasis upon educational "outcomes" can give sharper definition to the academic program and can assist an institution in identifying those experiences that seem to have the most positive influence upon students.

Students and Student Services

Colleges and universities should make efforts to involve students more effectively in the affairs of the institution.

Although not all students want to be involved in the governance structure of the institution, institutions and students can benefit by increased student participation in the affairs of the institution. Such involvement can contribute substantially to a greater sense of community on the campus, and is positive recognition of the important role undergraduates can play in campus affairs. Involvement in the governance process can contribute to students' understanding their academic work and the decision-making process. For many students it can provide an effective educational experience in itself, and a valuable on-campus practicum. "Involvement" does not just have to mean a few students being appointed to universitywide committees or serving on an advisory committee to the president of the institution. While these involvements may be useful, the most effective place for students to "become involved" with the institution is where they spend most of their time—with their own department and faculty. This "involvement" might simply mean getting to feel a part of the department by participating in the events of the department—whether social, academic, or recreational. This sense of community can be of great assistance to undergraduates in making them feel a part of the institution. Undergraduate education is most effective in its impact upon students when they feel a strong sense of identity with the college—as active academic colleagues with the faculty, not as passive, impersonal "consumers."

Institutions should initiate cocurricular programs that are consistent with their educational goals.

Usually, colleges and universities pay little attention to what students do in their own organizations and activities. Many students prefer it this way, and most faculty are not enthusiastic about "invading the private lives" of students or about returning to an *in loco parentis* relationship with students. However, if "student life" on the campus operates in isolation from faculty, the institution is missing an excellent opportunity to extend its educational influence. Most students are in class only about fifteen hours per week, and spend most of their time in other places on and off campus. Without trying to control the personal lives of these undergraduates, the institution can expand its educational program by planning and implementing cocurricular activities. Academic departments can invite various student organizations to participate in a variety of projects, whose nature can be academic, service, cultural, or recreational. Not only can such programs be useful in terms of academic and social benefits, but they also can increase the enjoyment that students have as undergraduates and can bring them into closer contact with faculty. Involvement in cocurricular programs can give undergraduates an opportunity to work together with faculty on important projects, to learn how to apply what they have been taught in actual problem-oriented situations. Although students can learn a great deal from each other, the college should not leave these matters entirely to chance. Through significant involvement with faculty on useful and stimulating projects, students' learning can be extended effectively beyond the classroom.

Colleges and universities should strive to develop student services programs that are integrated with academic departments.

Some student services programs, especially on large campuses, have contributed to the perception that the university is "just another bureaucracy" and that there is no real connection between one part of the campus and another. Counseling services, financial aid offices, and placement programs are too frequently isolated from academic departments, and faculty too often have little knowledge of these services. On-campus residences such as fraternities and sororities, cooperatives, and dormitories are usually "student ghettos" and usually have little relationship to overall academic programs. Many faculty have been teaching undergraduates on the same campus for several years, and have never even been inside these facilities. Many students also work at various campus jobs, but few institutions make adequate efforts to place their students in part-time employment related to their academic interests or career goals. Faculty serve as academic advisers to undergraduates, and their assistance in evaluating the campus employment of their advisees could contribute to more educationally effective student work programs. While college unions have traditionally been a place for students to relax and to engage in informal recreation, they have frequently not involved faculty members. Students often want to be alone and enjoy life with other students. However, student affairs administrators have not done enough to bring students and faculty together. Institutions should make strenuous efforts to integrate student services and academic programs. The false dichotomy that exists between the two programs only serves to bureaucratize the campus into isolated and noncommunicating groups.

Colleges and universities should include value development as an important educational goal.

Without attempting to indoctrinate all students with the same values or fit them into a "predetermined mold," institutions should make efforts to help students become aware of their own value positions, their origins, and their implications for decisionmaking. Students should know that the process of education at their institution is not "valuefree." Through course work, advising programs, residential arrangements, student-faculty relationships, and cocurricular programs, colleges and universities can be of real assistance to students in their value development. Students should realize that the educational goals of the institution represent a value position and should understand how and why these goals were selected. The institution should assist students gain an appreciation for the different value positions of other people, especially in different cultures. The relationship of a student's values to his/her personal and professional aspirations is an important educational concern for colleges and universities. Expressing such concern for students does not have to be an invasion of their privacy; it can be part of an authentic attempt to assist them in their educational development.

Colleges and universities should strive to accommodate the "new" students that increasingly are enrolling in higher education.

With the growing egalitarianism in American higher education, the students will be even more diverse in their social background, academic ability, learning styles, and expectations for education. These "new" students, described in some detail in Chapter 3, offer new challenges to colleges and universities in their undergraduate programs. For institutions to serve them well, significant adjustments may be necessary. Initially colleges and universities need to recognize these new students as an asset, not as an indication that their standards are "being lowered." Faculty with experience in working with very diverse students are needed; better and more individualized counseling programs should be developed. Instead of admitting only students who, at time of entrance, already have the characteristics the institution desires in its graduates, with the "new" students emphasis needs to be placed upon actual impact—the real educational progress that is made for the student over the period of time he or she is enrolled. These "new" students probably will not conform neatly to established institutional patterns, and may, for example, take longer to complete certain courses or, in fact, their entire undergraduate program. If an institution cannot develop sufficient flexibility to see such diverse needs, it undoubtedly will find that these "new" students will enroll elsewhere. None of this has to imply that the institution has to lower its academic standards—it means that the institution needs to create more diverse teaching methods, academic policies, and student services to assist these students meet their educational goals. It may be the increasing pressure of such students, more than any other factor, that stimulates institutions to rethink their programs in undergraduate education.

Index

Index

141

About the Author

Arthur Sandeen received the B.A. from Miami University at Oxford, Ohio, the M.A. and the Ph.D. from Michigan State University, the latter two in Administration and Higher Education. Dr. Sandeen is Vice-President for Student Affairs and Associate Professor of Educational Administration at the University of Florida. He has served as Dean of Students and Associate Professor of Education at Iowa State University and Director of Research for the National Association of Student Personnel Administrators.